Crossing Pedagogical Oceans:
International Teaching Assistants in U.S. Undergraduate Education

by Rosslyn M. Smith, Patricia Byrd, Gayle L. Nelson, Ralph Pat Barrett, and Janet C. Constantinides

ASHE-ERIC Higher Education Report No. 8, 1992

Prepared by

Clearinghouse on Higher Education
The George Washington University

In cooperation with

Association for the Study
of Higher Education

Published by

School of Education and Human Development
The George Washington University

Jonathan D. Fife, Series Editor

Cite as
Smith, Rosslyn M., and Patricia Byrd, Gayle L. Nelson, Ralph Pat Barrett, and Janet C. Constantinides. 1992. *Crossing Pedagogical Oceans: International Teaching Assistants in U.S. Undergraduate Education.* ASHE-ERIC Higher Education Report No. 8. Washington, D.C.: The George Washington University, School of Education and Human Development.

Library of Congress Catalog Card Number 93-83926
ISSN 0884-0040
ISBN 1-878380-21-4

Managing Editor: Bryan Hollister
Manuscript Editor: Alexandra Rockey
Cover design by Michael David Brown, Rockville, Maryland

The ERIC Clearinghouse on Higher Education invites individuals to submit proposals for writing monographs for the *ASHE-ERIC Higher Education Report* series. Proposals must include:
1. A detailed manuscript proposal of not more than five pages.
2. A chapter-by-chapter outline.
3. A 75-word summary to be used by several review committees for the initial screening and rating of each proposal.
4. A vita and a writing sample.

ERIC Clearinghouse on Higher Education
School of Education and Human Development
The George Washington University
One Dupont Circle, Suite 630
Washington, DC 20036-1183

This publication was prepared partially with funding from the Office of Educational Research and Improvement, U.S. Department of Education, under contract no. ED RI-88-062014. The opinions expressed in this report do not necessarily reflect the positions or policies of OERI or the Department.

Changing scientific and technical education demographics have led in the late 20th century to the appointment of significant numbers of international students as graduate teaching assistants at U.S. institutions. With many American students turning to careers that do not require graduate study, research universities have found that international students often are outstanding graduate students—and they often are better prepared in mathematics and other scientific and technical areas than their American peers.

For many U.S. students, parents, and academic and political leaders, the demographic change is viewed as part of the crisis in undergraduate education and the overvaluing of both graduate education and the research function of the university and its faculty. Critics call for the use of regular full-time faculty in undergraduate courses rather than graduate teaching assistants.

For other educators and political leaders, the increased presence of non-U.S. citizens implies a deflection of funding from American minority students. These critics support the use of graduate teaching assistants but would replace international students with American minority students.

While the debate about the basic purposes and methods of the research university continues, institutions have continued to appoint international graduate students to teach undergraduate courses. Although institutions may be interested in international educational exchange, the primary reason for selecting international teaching assistants (ITAs) is the continuing shortage of qualified American students.

What is the Legislative and Academy Response to Complaints About the Use of ITAs in Undergraduate Education?

In the 1970s and early 1980s, student complaints about ITAs appeared in articles in campus newspapers and in the national press. These complaints led some parents to pressure legislators and university administrators to take action to "do something" about the "international TA problem."

Since 1992, 18 states either have passed laws or implemented system-wide mandates to assess the language skills of ITAs. Some of these mandates also require ITAs to complete training programs or short courses to develop language and pedagogical skills. The academy, in turn, has responded by addressing this issue in professional meetings, journals, workshops, and seminars, as well as by establishing specialized programs for ITAs.

What Program Models Have Been Developed To Address the Training Needs of ITAs?

Although the specific features of individual programs vary widely, many fit the typology that categorizes ITA programs as *orientation, pre-term,* or *concurrent.*

Orientation programs are the shortest—lasting the equivalent of one to five days—and focus on the immediate survival and instructional needs of the ITAs. Pre-term models last from two to eight weeks in the summer preceding the fall term and are intensive in nature.

Concurrent programs occur during the regular terms but normally are not intensive. Pre-term and concurrent programs generally address aspects of communicative competence by including instruction in language skills, pedagogical skills, cross-cultural issues, and microteaching practice. Some programs focus on the discipline-specific as well as the cross-disciplinary needs of ITAs. No single design is the best for all institutions; the most effective programs take into account a thorough understanding of the structure, culture, and needs of the institution.

What Assessment Instruments Are Used To Screen and Evaluate ITAs?

Faculty and teaching assistants for years have been evaluated using various instruments such as student evaluations, peer evaluations, and self-evaluations. However, it became apparent that additional or modified instruments were needed to assess the linguistic and pedagogical skills of ITAs. These new or modified instruments include (1) commercially produced tests such as the Test of Spoken English and its locally administered version, the SPEAK test, (2) oral interviews, (3) oral communicative performance tests, and (4) teaching simulations. One or more of these instruments often are used to screen prospective ITAs prior to training, at the conclusion of the training program, or to "certify" for the classroom.

ITA programs are evaluated using several techniques, including:
- Undergraduate students' evaluations of ITAs;
- Surveys of ITA training program participants and staff;
- Surveys of the ITAs' department heads or supervisors; and

- Evaluations of the amount of progress made by students of the ITAs as measured by course grades.

What Type of Research has Supported and Informed ITA Training Program Design and Content?

Research in the form of dissertations and other quantitative and qualitative studies has focused on the areas of pronunciation, effective teaching, ITA training programs, the tasks ITAs perform, and the concerns of ITAs. Although this research has informed program design and implementation, many gaps exist within the knowledge base.

The research studies provide a relatively consistent pattern of factors related to ITA pronunciation and effective teaching behaviors, showing that pronunciation is only one of many factors influencing communication between ITAs and U.S. undergraduates. However, a broad spectrum of research is needed in the following additional areas:

1. The characteristics of the undergraduate classroom, including topics related to both general and discipline-specific teaching tasks and skills, the effects on students of internationalization and multiculturalism in the classroom, the level of English proficiency necessary for effective instruction, and the effectiveness as teachers of ITAs measured as a group compared to U.S. TAs measured as a group.
2. Methods and materials that facilitate successful ITA training and assessment, including the evaluation of cross-disciplinary and discipline-specific methods and materials, the evaluation of specific curricular components of training programs, the appropriateness of the testing systems and instruments that evaluate the linguistic, pedagogical, and cultural knowledge of ITAs, and the selection of assessment instruments that best fit a specific training program design.
3. The personal and professional results of training for international graduate students themselves, including the possible "Americanization" of the ITAs, and the cultural adjustment processes or internal conflicts experienced by the ITAs during their training program and subsequent classroom experiences.
4. The features of effective intercultural orientation for U.S. undergraduates, including their orientation to different cultures, to cultural and pedagogical differences in class-

room dynamics, to strategies for more effective learning from an ITA, and studies on how U.S. undergraduates might change over time as a result of exposure to ITAs and/or exposure to intercultural orientation.

5. Appropriate assessment and training for international faculty members, including the collection of data on how many non-native speakers of English now teach in U.S. colleges and universities and what subjects they teach, the characteristics of their relationships with undergraduates compared to those developed between ITAs and their undergraduate students, the political and legal ramifications of training and assessment for international faculty, and the nature of the assessment and training that should be made available to international faculty.

6. Policy planning issues, including how institutions define and identify ITAs, the impact of ITA training and assessment on institutional goals for internationalization and multiculturalism, strategic planning regarding the future role of ITAs in undergraduate instruction, and funding for assessment and training.

How Can University Administrators Support the Development and Implementation of ITA Training And Assessment Programs?

A successful ITA training program depends in large measure upon the quality and quantity of administrative support it receives. Administrators can support ITA training programs by (1) developing clearly defined, fair policies for assessing and training ITAs and implementing and enforcing these policies; (2) providing stable and adequate funding for the programs; and (3) supporting scholarship focusing on the various issues raised by ITA assessment and training.

Additionally, administrators should recognize and respect the needs and rights of ITAs as well as the undergraduate students they teach. Top administrators also must articulate both within and outside of the university community a balanced view of ITAs that acknowledges legitimate concerns without overlooking the important contributions to American universities that these international scholars make through their research and teaching.

The term *teaching assistant* (TA) refers to a graduate student who also holds a part-time instructional position in the university. This instruction can include lecturing, teaching a laboratory section, leading a discussion section, tutoring, and related duties. During the 1980s, two terms emerged to refer to international teaching assistants: foreign TAs and international TAs. Throughout this text, the current national practice of using *international TA* or *ITA* is followed.

The term *international teaching assistants* (ITAs) refers to TAs who are international graduate students holding non-immigrant visas, regardless of their first language. *International faculty* refers to faculty who are non-U.S. citizens or to those who were born in another country and became either U.S. citizens or permanent residents of the U.S. The definition of international faculty is more inclusive than the definition of ITA because of the relative permanence of faculty in their positions as compared to that of teaching assistants. The term *international faculty* does not refer to faculty who are U.S. citizens who have traveled abroad nor does it refer to non-native English-speaking U.S. citizens born in the United States.

ADVISORY BOARD

CONSULTING EDITORS

Philip Altbach
State University of New York–Buffalo

Louis Attinasi, Jr.
University of Houston

Margaret J. Barr
Texas Christian University

Beverly Belson
Western Michigan University

David W. Breneman
Harvard University

Kimberly Brown
Portland State University

Barbara B. Burn
University of Massachusetts–Amherst

L. Edwin Coate
Oregon State University

Robert Cope
Northwoods Institute

Dennis E. Gregory
Wake Forest University

Robert M. Hendrickson
The Pennsylvania State University

Mary Ann Heverly
Delaware County Community College

Malcolm D. Hill
The Pennsylvania State University

Clifford P. Hooker
University of Minnesota

Donald Kirby
Le Moyne College

George D. Kuh
Indiana University

Richard D. Lambert
Johns Hopkins University

Sock-Foon C. MacDougall
Bowie State University

REVIEW PANEL

Richard Duran
University of California

Kenneth C. Green
University of Southern California

Edward R. Hines
Illinois State University

Marsha W. Krotseng
West Virginia State College and University Systems

George D. Kuh
Indiana University–Bloomington

Daniel T. Layzell
University of Wisconsin System

Meredith Ludwig
American Association of State Colleges and Universities

Mantha V. Mehallis
Florida Atlantic University

Robert J. Menges
Northwestern University

Toby Milton
Essex Community College

James R. Mingle
State Higher Education Executive Officers

Gary Rhoades
University of Arizona

G. Jeremiah Ryan
Harford Community College

Daryl G. Smith
Claremont Graduate School

William Tierney
Pennsylvania State University

Susan Twombly
University of Kansas

Harold Wechsler
University of Rochester

Michael J. Worth
The George Washington University

CONTENTS

Foreword	**xvii**
Acknowledgments	**xix**

International Influences on U.S. Higher Education	**1**
Historical Background	1
Growth in International Student Population At U.S. Colleges and Universities	1
Decrease in U.S. Student Enrollments in Scientific and Technical Fields of Study	3
Points of Contact Between ITAs and U.S. Undergraduates	3
International Faculty at U.S. Colleges And Universities	9
Other "International" Influences on U.S. Colleges and Universities	9
Internationalization of U.S. Colleges And Universities	10
ITAs as Symbols: Intimations of Enduring Tensions In the Research University	11

Reactions to International Teaching Assistants	**15**
Public Response	15
Legislative Response	15
The Academy's Response	16

Training Programs for ITAs	**21**
TA Training as a Context for Training ITAs	21
Systems Analysis: Designing an Appropriate ITA Program	23
ITA Program Designs	27
Curricular Components	37
Implementation Issues	42
Programs for International Faculty	44

Assessment Issues in ITA Training	**47**
Assessment of TAs as a Context For ITA Assessment	47
ITA Assessment	51
ITA Training Models and How They are Used	58
Evaluation of Training Programs	62
Other Forms of Training Program Assessment	65
Summary	66

Research Related to ITA Training	**67**
Studies Related to Pronunciation	68
Studies Related to Effective Teaching	70
Studies Evaluating ITA Training Programs	75
Studies Related to Tasks ITAs Perform	78
Studies Related to the Concerns of ITAs	78
Summary	79

Conclusion	**81**
Topics Needing Further Discussion and Research	82
Required Administrative Support for Effective ITA	
Assessment and Training Programs	85
The Future of ITA Assessment and Training	86
References	**89**
Index	**112**

FOREWORD

The use of graduate students to teach undergraduate students has been a part of American higher education since Johns Hopkins University was founded and the research university was born. The contributions these teaching assistants, or TAs, make to the institution's instructional process are many. They allow for an economy of scale that makes it financially possible for large lecture classes also to have small discussion sessions; the TAs' enthusiasm for their graduate studies and research can be contagious; and, often, graduate students can personally relate more easily to undergraduate students. However, as undergraduate students, their parents, and others become more critical consumers, there has been increased dissatisfaction voiced concerning the effectiveness of TAs, especially those who come from other countries.

In many cases, the issues surrounding international teaching assistants, or ITAs, are the same as those that are applicable to American TAs, with two major differences: language and cultural competencies. Because these differences are most noticeable, they generate the most vocal concern. However, in many cases the failure of the institution to ensure that the ITAs have been trained to teach effectively is only symptomatic of the limited training process that exists for all TAs. Therefore, the steps that institutions are now taking to ensure the effectiveness of ITAs also is very applicable to all TAs.

The use of ITAs by research universities has almost become an unavoidable necessity. First, there are many academic areas that attract a large number of international students and fewer U.S. students. It is only natural that a significant number of the brightest of these students who apply to be TAs will be international students. Increasingly, institutions find that the use of ITAs helps to add a very desirable international dimension that previously was lacking in a course. The basic conclusion is that the use of TAs, regardless if they are U.S. or international graduate students, is desirable both for pedagogical and financial reasons. However, as institutions continue to use TAs, the institutions must take increased measures to ensure that TAs are well-trained and effective instructors.

The increased use of ITAs and student and public concern over ITA teaching effectiveness is forcing institutions to reexamine their policies and practices regarding TAs in general and ITAs specifically. In this report by Rosslyn M. Smith, professor at Texas Tech University; Patricia Byrd, associate professor at Georgia State University; Gayle L. Nelson, assistant professor at Georgia State University; Ralph Pat Barrett, former professor at Michigan State University; and Janet C. Constantinides, professor at the University of Wyoming, the literature and institutional practices concerning ITAs are comprehensively reviewed. After examining the growth of international influences on U.S. higher education, the authors present a detailed accounting of current institutional training programs for ITAs, the research that is available relating to this training, and the assessment issues in ITA training.

Over the course of the next decade, most—if not all—undergraduate programs will use international students as TAs. As institutions are held more accountable for the quality and effectiveness of their teaching process, the training of TAs, especially ITAs, will become a major concern. This report reviews the positions of institutions today and provides guidance for their positions in the future.

Jonathan D. Fife
Series Editor, Professor of Higher Education Administration, and Director, ERIC Clearinghouse on Higher Education
The George Washington University

ACKNOWLEDGMENTS

The authors gratefully acknowledge the reviewers for their in-depth comments and suggestions on an earlier version of this manuscript.

INTERNATIONAL INFLUENCES ON U.S. HIGHER EDUCATION

Historical Background

The development of the American research university in the late 19th century involved grafting the German concept of graduate and professional education onto the basic stock of the English system of liberal art education for undergraduates (Boyer 1991; Gruber 1975; Veysey 1965). The combination was modified by the American context into a system of state and regional, rather than national, institutions that are highly aware of and responsive to the educational and economic needs of their particular settings (Gruber 1975).

These sources of tension continue in the late 20th century to be central to discussions about a very new problem for U.S. research universities. . . .

From the beginning, U.S. research universities have struggled with unresolved contradictions in this structure, including:

1. Arguments over the relative value and status given to graduate in contrast to undergraduate education;
2. Disagreements about the relative merits of research and teaching;
3. Discord within the university over demands for changes made by various constituencies outside the university; and
4. Struggles for control of institutional purposes, values, and resources between faculty and administration (Gruber 1975; Veysey 1965).

These sources of tension continue in the late 20th century to be central to discussions about a very new problem for U.S. research universities—their growing dependence on international graduate students to teach courses in the undergraduate curriculum.

Growth in International Student Population
At U.S. Colleges and Universities

Since World War II, higher education in the United States has rapidly expanded to meet the needs of an ever more diverse student body and faculty. As a result of the influx of students and faculty from non-English and non-Western backgrounds, college and university faculty and staff are being asked to meet needs that are still in the process of being understood (Coombs 1985; Hoekje and Williams 1992).

The surge in the number of students from the People's Republic of China (PRC) illustrates the dimensions of the change: In late 1978, only 50 students from the PRC were enrolled in U.S. institutions of higher education (Burn 1980).

In 1991, 39,600 students from the PRC were attending U.S. colleges and universities (Mangan 1992a). In the fall term of 1991 at one major research university, 10 of 11 new students in the graduate program in physics were from the PRC.

The increase in the numbers of PRC students reflects two trends in U.S. higher education: (1) a general increase in the numbers of international students and (2) a decrease in the numbers of U.S. students entering graduate programs in science, technology, and business administration.

Open Doors, the report of an annual survey of international students in the United States published by the Institute of International Education, first was issued in 1955. For the academic year 1954-55, the survey found that 34,232 international students were studying in the United States. Of these, 19,124 were undergraduates; 12,110 were graduates; 2,205 had special status; 793 did not report an academic status for the survey (*Open Doors* 1955).

By the academic year 1984-85, 338,894 international students were in the United States with 122,590 in graduate programs (*Open Doors* 1985). In 1990-91, 407,500 international students were at institutions of higher learning in the United States with 182,100 in graduate school, compared with 189,900 undergraduates (Dodge 1991; *Open Doors* 1991). The trend through the 1980s and into the 1990s was a greater increase in the graduate than the undergraduate population of international students. Therefore, the actual number of graduate students was expected to be equal to or to exceed the undergraduate population by the mid-1990s (Chandler 1989; *Open Doors* 1991).

In addition to its influence on the student population, this change has had profound influence on the makeup of the faculties of U.S. colleges and universities. It has led to rapid increases in the numbers of graduate teaching assistants and regular faculty members who are native speakers of languages other than English and who come from non-U.S. and non-Western cultural and educational traditions (National Research Council 1988):

A disproportionately large number [of foreign-born engineering students] come from countries where the language and cultural backgrounds are likely to be significantly different from those of most native-born Americans. In 1985, for example, 31 percent of the foreign engineering students in U.S. schools came from the Far East, 6 percent from India, and 20 percent from the Middle East (p. 3).

Decrease in U.S. Student Enrollments In Scientific and Technical Fields of Study

At the same time that the numbers of international students were increasing in U.S. graduate schools, the numbers of Americans studying for advanced degrees were decreasing, especially in business administration, engineering, the lab sciences, and other scientific and technological areas (Chandler 1989; Mooney 1990). For example, in the past 20 years, the number of U.S. citizens receiving doctorates in mathematics has decreased by 50 percent; in 1989, most of the Ph.D.s in mathematics awarded by U.S. universities went to citizens of other countries (*Everybody* 1989).

Like mathematics, engineering has seen a dramatic decrease in the numbers of U.S. students at all levels of higher education, but most especially in graduate programs (National Research Council 1988):

> . . . *the proportion of foreign assistant professors of engineering younger than age 35 has increased from 10 percent in 1972 to over 50 percent during the period 1983-85. About two-thirds of the postdoctoral university appointees are not U.S. citizens. Also, the number of foreign applicants for graduate students in engineering is greater than the number of U.S. applicants, and about 60 percent of foreign students obtaining Ph.D. degrees in the United States remain here. Over 90 percent of undergraduates in engineering but only about 45 percent of new engineering Ph.D.s are U.S. citizens (about 4 percent of this latter group were naturalized citizens)* (p. 2).

Points of Contact Between ITAs and U.S. Undergraduates

While the number of international students certainly has grown rapidly and while the percentage of international graduate students has increased in certain fields, international students remain a small percentage of the total U.S. student body (Kerr 1980). In France, for example, international students make up 12.5 percent of the total student body in higher education. In the United States, these students are only 2.5 percent of the total number of students in college and university programs (Chandler 1989).

In spite of these relatively small numbers in the total population, the perception that ITAs are having a significant impact on U.S. undergraduate education has led to the responses delineated by the present study. To date, no study has been completed to detail the actual numbers of international students and scholars with roles as teachers in U.S. higher education. Major problems will hamper any attempt to carry out such a study. Such problems might include the difficulty of settling on definitions of "international" (Are only the individuals who are on non-immigrant visas to be counted?) and of "teacher" (Are lab assistants counted, and are regular faculty considered along with graduate teaching assistants?).

International graduate students come from many different countries and seem to teach in a wide variety of disciplines including education, foreign languages, the arts, and the social sciences. Many ITAs reportedly are well-received by their students and provide high-quality instruction (e.g., R. Smith and Slusher 1988).

Concern about the communication and teaching skills of ITAs seems most acute when ITAs from non-native English-speaking or non-Western backgrounds teach basic required courses that are used for screening entrance into business, scientific, and technical fields of study. Since data are not yet available on the numbers of ITAs in U.S. universities, their fields of study, and the courses they teach, the influence of ITAs on undergraduate students can be approached only indirectly from two perspectives.

The data regarding fields of study that have shown a large increase in graduate international student enrollment and a decrease in graduate U.S. student enrollment (e.g., Chandler 1989; *Everybody* 1989; Mooney 1990; National Research Council 1988) suggest that ITAs are especially likely to teach courses in business administration, mathematics, laboratory sciences, engineering, and other scientific and technological areas. Clearly, the specific disciplines and the numbers of ITAs teaching in each will vary from year to year and from institution to institution.

If this inference is correct, then it follows that additional indirect evidence about the contact between international TAs and U.S. undergraduates may be adduced by considering the numbers of U.S. students taking those courses likely to be taught by ITAs. Adelman gives details on the transcripts of students in a national sample of 12,600 students who completed high school in 1972 and are continuing to participate in a study of the educational preparation and experience of U.S. citizens (1990).

This study uses information from 1972 to 1984 to trace the educational history of the students in the sample and to show the patterns that exist in U.S. higher education. Adelman provides two important types of information that can be the basis for analyzing the contacts between U.S. undergraduates and ITAs. First, he enumerates the courses and fields of study most often chosen by undergraduates. Second, he describes the types of institutions at which the courses are taken, an important indicator of the likelihood of contact with ITAs, since research and comprehensive universities are more likely to be using international graduate students as teachers than are liberal arts colleges or community colleges.

Table 1 lists courses that were taken by more than 20 percent of students in Adelman's sample who completed a bachelor's degree. Of the 21 courses most frequently taken by undergraduates, seven are among those most likely to be taught by international TAs. These include biology, statistics, and calculus, which are "gatekeeping" courses that frequently are used to limit the number of students who can enter many technical and scientific fields, including medicine, engineering, and business administration (*Everybody* 1989; Steen 1987).

Adelman aggregated the particular courses taken by undergraduates into "fields of study" (1990). Table 2 shows the fields taken by 20 percent or more of the students in the sample. Of these 28 "fields of study," undergraduates are most likely to encounter ITAs in 10. Again, these "fields" often are used as prerequisites for certain majors and, ultimately, for entry into particular areas of graduate and professional study.

In addition to providing details on the courses and fields of study of U.S. undergraduates, Adelman analyzes the types of institutions at which the study occurred using six categories: doctoral, comprehensive, liberal arts, community college, trade, and specialized (medical or law schools, for example) (1990). The data provided by Adelman indicate that courses in mathematics, statistics, chemistry, and physics were taken primarily at doctoral or comprehensive universities—contexts in which students are most likely to take such courses from ITAs.

TABLE 1

COURSES TAKEN BY 20% OR MORE OF STUDENTS IN SAMPLE*

Course Title	Percentage of Sample Taking the Course
1. Intro. Accounting	**22.6**
2. Communications: General	35.6
3. Educational Psychology	21.9
4. Literature: General/Intro	30.9
5. Freshman Composition	72.7
6. American Literature	23.0
7. Biology: General	**46.7**
8. Statistics, Probability	**23.1**
9. Calculus, Different Equat	**30.4**
10. Physical Education Activities	66.5
11. Philosophy, Philosophical Problems	22.8
12. Chemistry: General	**35.3**
13. Physics: General	**26.2**
14. Psychology: General, Introduction	69.5
15. Developmental Psychology	35.9
16. Economics: Principles, Introduction	**44.1**
17. World History/Western Civilization	29.2
18. U.S. History Surveys	41.9
19. U.S. Government & Politics	35.5
20. Sociology: Introduction, General	9.5
21. Art History & Appreciation	22.1

*Adapted from Adelman (1990), pp. 141-60. Bold type marks courses in business, scientific, and technical fields that are often taught by ITAs.

Table 3 shows the percentage of courses for these subjects taken at the various types of institutions. For example, 4,558 students presented transcripts with "Physics: General" (Adelman 1990, p. 221). Because of the limited number of Americans pursuing graduate degrees in physics, research and comprehensive universities are very likely to rely on ITAs to teach introductory physics and physics labs.

In sum, the majority of U.S. undergraduates are likely to have comparatively limited but intensely important contact with ITAs. Undergraduates will take most of their courses with instructors who are native speakers of English ("Full-Time" 1991). However, many undergraduates will take required courses in mathematics, statistics, chemistry, and physics from

TABLE 2

PERCENTAGE OF STUDENTS IN SAMPLE TAKING COURSES IN CERTAIN FIELDS OF STUDY*

Field of Study	Percentage
1. Accounting	**23.8**
2. Business Administration	**33.3**
3. Education: Other	22.1
4. Biological Sciences: General	**36.3**
5. Soil Science: All Other	27.7
6. Chemistry	**29.0**
7. Physical Sciences: All Other	**20.3**
8. Pre-College Mathematics [includes "pre-collegiate math"]	**32.9**
9. Introduction to College Mathematics	**30.9**
10. Calculus/Advanced Mathematics	**21.0**
11. Liberal & Interdisciplinary [courses in the humanities/social sciences]	24.2
12. Foreign Languages: Elem/Int	26.6
13. Literature/Letters	51.8
14. Philosophy	31.1
15. World/West Civilization	21.9
16. U.S. History Surveys	32.0
17. History: All Other	26.0
18. U.S. Government	26.2
19. Writing Skills [includes remedial/developmental language]: All	75.2
20. Communication: Introduction	29.4
21. Communication: All Other	25.5
22. Psychology: General	56.5
23. Psychology: All Other	27.1
24. Sociology: Introduction	39.2
25. Sociology: All Other	25.1
26. Economics: Introduction	**31.4**
27. Music: All Other	23.7
28. Physical and Health Activities	61.2

*Adapted from Adelman (1990), pp. 167-70. Bold type marks courses in business, scientific, and technical fields often taught by ITAs.

instructors who are non-native speakers of English, many of whom have little experience with U.S. culture or U.S. education. R. Lambert notes that a current, common practice in the sciences is to hire new international students as TAs or lab assistants, which "almost assures that they will be in front of the classroom when their English skills are most limited" (1993, p. 7).

TABLE 3

PERCENTAGE OF COURSES TAKEN BY INSTITUTION TYPE*

Course/Institution Type	Percentage
"Pre-collegiate Math: General"	
Doctoral	*17.2*
Comprehensive	*42.0*
Liberal Arts	5.5
Community College	33.6
Trade	1.2
Specialized	0.4
"Calculus, Differential Equations"	
Doctoral	*44.0*
Comprehensive	*30.9*
Liberal Arts	6.0
Community College	12.9
Trade	0.3
Specialized	5.7
"Statistics, Probability"	
Doctoral	*36.7*
Comprehensive	*39.4*
Liberal Arts	6.5
Community College	13.3
Trade	0.2
Specialized	4.0
"Chemistry: General"	
Doctoral	*37.8*
Comprehensive	*33.0*
Liberal Arts	4.9
Community College	19.5
Trade	1.0
Specialized	3.7
"Organic Chemistry"	
Doctoral	*52.9*
Comprehensive	*33.0*
Liberal Arts	5.7
Community College	6.9
Trade	0.2
Specialized	1.3
"Physics: General"	
Doctoral	*42.1*
Comprehensive	*31.3*
Liberal Arts	5.4
Community College	14.3
Trade	0.9
Specialized	6.1

*Adapted from Adelman (1990), pp. 211-12, 219, 221.

International Faculty at U.S. Colleges and Universities

While most attention has been given to the use of ITAs at research universities, many other types of colleges and universities are hiring greater numbers of faculty members of non-English and non-U.S. backgrounds. In the academic year 1954-55, approximately 635 foreigners held faculty positions at U.S. colleges and universities (*Open Doors* 1955). Three hundred thirty-six came from Europe; 20 percent were from the United Kingdom. Thirty-one percent taught natural and physical science; 23 percent, humanities; 22 percent, medicine; 11 percent, social sciences; 7 percent, engineering; 4 percent, education; and 2 percent, agriculture (*Open Doors* 1955).

By 1987, graduates of foreign universities made up substantial percentages of the full-time assistant professors in U.S. doctorate-granting institutions: 40 percent of the assistant professors teaching mathematics, 35 percent of the assistant professors teaching engineering, and 20 percent for science courses in general (*Everybody* 1989). The American Society for Engineering Education reported in 1987 that more than 50 percent of the faculty in some areas of engineering were foreign nationals. The United Kingdom still sends professors to the U.S., but the dominant region is Asia, with substantial numbers of faculty members who were originally from China, South Korea, and India joining the U.S. professoriate.

Other "International" Influences on U.S. Colleges and Universities

While this "foreign" influence was growing, the U.S. also was experiencing an increase in its refugee and immigrant population, especially from non-European sources. Refugees have arrived from around the world, seeking shelter from the political upheavals in their home countries. For example, major refugee groups in the U.S. include the Cambodian, Cuban, Ethiopian, Haitian, Russian, and Vietnamese communities.

Immigrants, especially those from India, South Korea, and Taiwan, have brought new wealth to the U.S. as they seek economic and educational advantages for their families. The growth of these communities in Atlanta, as one major U.S. city, illustrates changes taking place across the United States. It is estimated that 10 percent of the inhabitants of Atlanta were born outside the United States ("Today's" 1992).

In 1992, Atlanta was home to more than 100,000 Hispanics, 30,000 Chinese, 25,000 Koreans, 10,000 Indians, 5,000 Eritreans, 4,200 Japanese, 4,000 Vietnamese, 2,000 Thais, and 2,000 Hmong ("Today's" 1992). The children of these communities are now finishing U.S. high schools and entering U.S. colleges and universities in substantial numbers. Faculty and staff may find it difficult—if not impossible—to distinguish the "foreign" student from the "native" student when both are non-native speakers of English and especially when they are from non-European backgrounds. Both strands seem to merge together as these students move into and through the university, earning undergraduate degrees, finishing graduate and professional programs, and even joining the faculty.

Internationalization of U.S. Colleges and Universities
While "diversity" seems to be overtaking it as a theme, "internationalization" remains a topic of importance for many administrators and faculty members at U.S. colleges and universities (S.K. Bailey 1977; Burn 1980; Greenfield 1990; Harari 1983; Kerr 1980; National Research Council 1987; Pickert 1991). Discussions of "internationalization," however, primarily treat the need to provide experiences outside the United States for U.S. students, faculty, and administrators. When international students and faculty are included in these discussions, the focus is on the need to provide special services for international students and to use them as resources in changing the attitudes and increasing the knowledge of U.S. students (e.g., H. Jenkins 1983; Kerr 1980; Lee, Abd-Ella, and Burks 1981; Pickert 1991) rather than delving into any influence that international students and faculty might have had on the curriculum, programs, and governance of U.S. colleges and universities.

There are signs that changes are occurring in U.S. higher education to accommodate international students and students from non-English backgrounds who are U.S. residents. For example, course adjustments are being made to make the content more relevant to the needs of these students. Will discusses changes that he made in his political science course to meet the specific needs of international students who had little previous knowledge of the U.S. political system (1980).

Numerous English departments offer special sections of freshman composition for students who are not native speakers of English. A major publisher provides a parallel version of its technical writing textbook aimed at the needs of non-native speakers of English—a sign that a market exists for such texts (Olsen and Huckin 1991).

A more pervasive change that points to internationalization of U.S. research universities is the topic of this book: the recognition by research universities of the influence international graduate students have on undergraduate education. Around the U.S., many research universities are changing their selection processes for graduate teaching assistants to include assessment and training for non-native speakers of English who are to be teachers of U.S. undergraduates.

It can be argued that "internationalization" of the U.S. research university already has begun—not by sending U.S. students and faculty overseas but rather by bringing increasing numbers of non-U.S. citizens or recent U.S. residents into positions of influence through their teaching, most notably of required introductory courses in business administration, mathematics, the hard sciences, and statistics.

The recognition by research universities of the influence international graduate students have on undergraduate education [is the topic of this book].

ITAs as Symbols: Intimations of Enduring Tensions In the Research University

The four unresolved tensions within U.S. research universities listed earlier can be seen running as themes through discussions of the use of ITAs to teach undergraduate courses (e.g., Cage 1991). The old topics take these new forms: (1) arguments over the relative value and status given to graduate in contrast to undergraduate education now include concerns about the use of ITAs; if undergraduate education is the central responsibility of a university, regular faculty should be teaching undergraduates rather than focusing their attention on graduate courses and research activities. Graduate students, especially those from overseas, should not be the teachers of undergraduates.

Thus, the related argument over (2) the relative merits of research and teaching is brought into the discussion along with a sub-theme about the selection of graduate teaching assistants on the basis of their academic, rather than their pedagogical, excellence. This argument about the purpose of the institution involves not just faculty members and administrators but the larger audience outside the institution that has influence over the institution through control of enrollment and of other funding.

Morris asserts that U.S. research institutions are discriminating against African-American doctoral students by providing them with less financial support than is provided for international doctoral students (1991). Other leaders of U.S. academic programs provided different interpretations of the facts (DePalma 1992), and the debate was featured in the letters to the editor section of the *New York Times* on May 12, 1992, with letters from four academics and the president-elect of the American Immigration Lawyers Association. The controversy drew attention to the place of international students in U.S. graduate programs, leading to the proposal of legislation to require the hiring of African-American students in federally funded research projects and to limit the number of internationals who could be funded through such projects.

Anecdotal evidence also suggests concerns in some quarters about the possible adverse influence of ITAs on U.S. students, especially women and minorities, wishing to enter professional, scientific, and technical fields of study. Some people, including academic administrators, are concerned that ITAs, who often teach required introductory courses that serve as barriers to entry into scientific and technical fields of study, have been given perhaps excessive power over which students enter graduate and professional programs in the U.S.

The concerns about women and minority students grow out of the importance for the U.S. of encouraging these students to develop adequate backgrounds in mathematics and the sciences. Those who hold this point of view note that some ITAs come from cultures in which women and minority students are not encouraged or even permitted to seek scientific or technical education. They wonder if ITAs from these types of cultural backgrounds can provide the supportive and encouraging environment needed for women and minority students to enter these fields of study in the greatly increased numbers needed by U.S. society.

These outside voices are reminders to those inside the university of a third recurring theme: (3) discord within the university over demands for changes made by various constituencies outside the university. Finally, the need to respond to those demands for change in priorities and methods often involves (4) a struggle between faculty and the central administration of the university over control of institutional purposes, values, and resources. Faculty generally are not accustomed to having decisions about their graduate students made by administrators or faculty members from other divisions of the institution (Rouvalis 1986). Thus, although some faculty welcome the services provided by an ITA program, the establishment of training programs for ITAs can, as a result of this struggle between faculty and administration, lead to tensions between faculty members and those given responsibility for assessment and training of ITAs.

In this complex environment, U.S. research universities continue to admit international graduate students and to fund them by hiring them to teach undergraduate courses as graduate teaching assistants. The intense emotions that often are aroused over the use of ITAs and international faculty to teach undergraduates seem to result not just from issues of linguistic and cultural competence of these foreigners as teachers of U.S. students. The strong opinions expressed on all sides of the issue reveal deep-seated tensions within the institution and between the institution and those who control the provision of its resources.

The remainder of this report details the changes that some university systems and individual institutions are making to resolve the tensions over this issue through the recognition of the problem and the development of assessment and training programs to improve the effectiveness of international teaching assistants and international faculty in their interactions with U.S. undergraduates.

REACTIONS TO INTERNATIONAL TEACHING ASSISTANTS

Public Response

A public outcry began in the late 1970s about the problems attributed to situations in which international graduate students serve as teaching assistants. Parents demanded to know if their children would have international TAs, making it clear to institutions that they did not want to send their students to institutions that used ITAs in introductory classes.

Trustees and college presidents found themselves facing questions about why any non-native speakers of English were allowed to teach undergraduate classes. In some cases, parents even suggested that teaching assistantships should be awarded only to Americans and, in the case of state universities, preferably to residents of that state (K. Bailey 1984). K. Bailey surveyed some of the complaints by undergraduate students and parents, most of which focused on language (1984). Such complaints were often published in newspaper articles bemoaning the poor language skills of international instructors. Many of the earliest stories appeared in student newspapers on college campuses (Elder 1977; Linnen 1977; Rosen 1977; Shaw 1982).

Student organizations addressed both the extent of the problem and ways to deal with it, including instituting "screening tests" ("Efforts" 1988; Swanbeck 1981; "UI Senate" 1986). Usually the complaints were directed toward ITAs, but in some cases international faculty also were the target of the complaints (Timmerman 1981). Such articles continue to appear in student newspapers (Creswell 1990).

In the early 1980s, the national press also featured stories about ITAs (Kelley 1982). By 1985, the subject of ITAs was found in the educationally related press as well (Fiske 1985; E.C. Gottschalk 1985; Heller 1985; "Let's Talk" 1985; McMillen 1986; Secter 1987). These stories sometimes mentioned that there had been attempts on campuses to deal with the problem. However, the emphasis usually was on the fact that there was a problem, most often identified as poor English skills—especially pronunciation.

Legislative Response

When the outcry became strident, legislatures reacted by mandating testing for international TAs and sometimes for international faculty as well. The first state to pass such legislation was Oklahoma, in 1982, requiring each college or university of the state system to devise procedures "to guarantee faculty members have proficiency in both written and spoken

English" (Oklahoma English Proficiency Act of 1982). In 1983, Florida passed a bill requiring that all faculty in the state university system, except people who teach a foreign language, must attain a given score on the *Test of Spoken English* (TSE) or similar test approved by the board of regents (Florida English Language Proficiency Act of 1983).

In Ohio, a state representative whose daughter had complained of her inability to understand an ITA introduced a bill to mandate oral English language proficiency testing (Molotsky 1985); House Bill 497 was passed in 1986. As of 1992, 14 states had legislation (California, Florida, Illinois, Iowa, Louisiana, Minnesota, Missouri, North Dakota, Ohio, Oklahoma, Pennsylvania, South Carolina, Tennessee, Texas). Additionally, four states had a higher education system-wide mandate on oral English language proficiency for teaching assistants (Arizona, Georgia, Kansas, Oregon). A typical mandate has four characteristics: (1) It is directed at universities rather than state-wide governing boards; (2) it focuses on non-native rather than native speakers; (3) it mandates assessment only of oral English language proficiency and ignores other pedagogical skills; and (4) it requires remediation of non-proficient instructors (Thomas and Monoson 1991). Seven of the 18 states (Florida, Illinois, North Dakota, Oklahoma, Pennsylvania, Tennessee, Texas) also require testing for regular faculty (Monoson and Thomas 1991). Indications are that other states also may mandate oral English language proficiency testing, since the influx of international graduate students continues to increase (*Open Doors* 1990).

But in many cases, testing is all that is required; only seven of the states (California, Illinois, Minnesota, North Dakota, Ohio, Oklahoma, Texas) require any training or "remediation" (Thomas and Monoson 1991). The implication seems to be that speaking English to some standard, often not defined, is a minimal qualification for employment as a teacher. This has legal implications (Brown, Fishman, and Jones 1990). It has been suggested that ITAs, and international faculty as well, may have recourse to law if the testing of their English proficiency as a condition of their employment is deemed discriminatory (Brown, Fishman, and Jones 1991).

The Academy's Response
Even before the spate of legislative requirements that mark the mid 1980s, individual institutions and professional organi-

zations were responding to the complaints by students and the public and were attempting to meet the needs of the international faculty and TAs and the American undergraduate students.

Professional organizations
The testing and training of international TAs became the subject of presentations at professional conferences. Organizations such as NAFSA (National Association for Foreign Student Affairs, now NAFSA: Association of International Educators) and TESOL (Teachers of English to Speakers of Other Languages) had sessions at their annual meetings by 1983, with more sessions appearing on the programs in each succeeding year (e.g., Puhl, Finger, and Barnes 1983; Turitz 1984; Constantinides 1985, 1987c; R. Smith, Constantinides, and Hudson 1989).

Both of these professional organizations for teachers of English as a Second Language (ESL) were among the earliest to become involved, because the ITA problem was (and sometimes still is) characterized as a problem with English. Thus, ESL teachers were among the first to be involved in the early training programs, many of which had only a language component.

Other professional organizations whose members were involved in other ways with international teaching assistants also began to include sessions on the subject in their meetings. SIETAR (Society for Intercultural Education, Training, and Research) and CGS (Council of Graduate Schools) sometimes even highlighted such sessions in their programs (Constantinides 1987b, 1988a, 1988b). In addition, items about ITA-related matters found their way into the official publications of professional societies such as the American Association of University Professors (AAUP), TESOL, and NAFSA (Ard and Swales 1986; Constantinides and Byrd 1986; Costantino 1986; Molotsky 1985; Parsons and Szelagowski 1983; Soppelsa 1985). As members of these professional organizations became involved in ITA training, somewhat more attention was given to matters of cross-cultural communication and pedagogy, so that many training programs now include those two components along with a language component.

Many believed that conference sessions did not provide enough time for in-depth consideration of the issues at hand, so longer meetings, conferences, and institutes were founded. In 1985, NAFSA organized a seminar on international teaching assistants that was held in Atlanta.

In 1986, the first national conference on teaching assistants was held at Ohio State University, sponsored by a variety of professional organizations including the Council on Graduate Schools, the Professional and Organization Development (POD) Network in Higher Education, the American Association for Higher Education, and NAFSA, and supported by the Lilly Endowment, Inc. A large number of presentations at that conference dealt with ITA issues, as distinct from the issues of TAs in general. In the proceedings of that conference, one section titled "International Teaching Assistants" contains 15 selections on ITA issues, ranging from program design models to testing procedures (Chism and Warner 1987).

In the two succeeding national conferences on teaching assistants, in Seattle in 1989 and Austin, Texas, in 1991, a specific segment of the programming focused on ITA issues. The publication that resulted from the Seattle conference (Nyquist, Abbott, Wulff, and Sprague 1991) again had a special section, "The International Teaching Assistant," with 14 papers included, adding topics such as state mandates for testing and training and discussion of discipline-specific training. A publication from the Austin conference is expected.

In preparation for the Seattle conference, a previous publication on TA training in the Jossey-Bass New Directions in Teaching and Learning series was updated, with two chapters specifically devoted to ITAs (Nyquist, Abbott, and Wulff 1989).

At least one conference has focused entirely on ITAs: the Symposium on International Teaching Assistants, held at the University of Pennsylvania in 1988. It was organized in response to a need for more opportunities to explore the problem and develop possible solutions than were available at the 1986 national TA conference. Selected papers from this symposium appear in a special issue of *English for Specific Purposes* (Young 1989).

As a result of the NAFSA seminar in 1985, a national summer institute was initiated in 1986. The Wyoming Institute on Foreign TA Training (later, the Wyoming/NAFSA Institute) was held each summer for four years. Sessions were offered to educators and administrators whose institutions were beginning or considering beginning ITA training-testing programs; other sessions were held for those who had some experience in the field already. Two sets of working papers were produced from the institutes, representing at the time the largest body of information on ITA testing and training available in one place (Constantinides 1986, 1987d).

In 1989, the first all-day pre-conference symposium on ITAs took place as part of the national TESOL convention. This symposium, which features between 11 and 15 presenters, has been a part of each subsequent convention.

Additionally, publications addressing various issues in ITA assessment and training appeared. In 1984, NAFSA published *Foreign Teaching Assistants in American Universities*. That volume identified the issues that have been the focus of many of the later publications: The Problem, The Programs, and The Progress (K. Bailey, Pialorsi, and Zukowski-Faust 1984).

In addition to the articles in journals and the presentations at professional meetings, texts, manuals, and videos have been produced for use in ITA training programs. A 1990 annotated bibliography (Briggs, Hyon, Aldridge, and Swales 1990) lists 10 items in this category. Madden and Myers (forthcoming) edited a collection of 12 articles on the discourse and performance of ITAs in a variety of contexts; the volume is devoted entirely to language and teaching research.

Another measure of the extent to which problems associated with ITAs have been accepted as legitimate subjects for consideration is the fact that Ph.D. dissertations have been written about them. By 1990, at least 16 dissertations had been produced (Briggs et al. 1990).

Studying the problem is not all that the academy has accomplished; it also has tried to look at how American undergraduates can be helped to cope more effectively with ITAs as class, lab, and discussion session instructors. In some cases, special programs, materials, or publications were created to sensitize the American undergraduate to the cultural and language differences they might expect to encounter if they have an international TA or faculty member (R. Smith, Constantinides, and Hudson 1989; R. Smith and Slusher 1988; vom Saal 1987).

Institutional responses

Individual institutions have responded to the ITA problem in a variety of ways. Some institutions have, seemingly, chosen to ignore the issue; it is difficult to assess this type of response, since the institutions in this category have not reported on their decisions. Many of those who have developed testing and/or training programs have reported on their efforts at the conferences discussed above and in the publications resulting from such conferences (Civikly and Muchisky 1991; Ford, Gappa, Wendorff, and Wright 1991; Lay and Mantel 1987; Schneider and Stevens 1991; Sequeira and Darling 1987; R. Smith 1987).

Because of the complaints, not only from students and parents but also from faculty who objected to institution-wide policies regarding the selection of ITAs, institutions began to produce "policy papers" for dissemination. Such papers explained the rationale behind employing ITAs or the measures the institution was taking to screen and train them, or both (e.g., "Answers" 1988).

Faculty object to mandated policies, whether from legislatures, higher education systems, or individual institutions. Faculty see such policies as interfering with each department's perceived right to control graduate student admission and assignment of tasks, including teaching, to these graduate students (Rouvalis 1986).

Institutions resent legislative mandates about testing and training ITAs and international faculty, because the institutions perceive such legislation as unwarranted intervention into operations. Consequently, administrators at research universities often find themselves facing criticism from students, parents, legislatures, and their own faculty. Such criticism may focus on any policy, or even lack thereof, the institution may have regarding international teaching assistants and faculty. Nonetheless, some university systems and individual institutions have acknowledged the complaints and criticism and have responded by developing assessment and training programs to meet the particular needs of ITAs (Mangan 1992b).

TRAINING PROGRAMS FOR ITAs

TA Training as a Context for Training ITAs

During the last 20 years, faculty and TA training programs in the United States have focused on classroom instruction. In many ways, the 1970s was the decade of faculty development, including training, and the 1980s was the decade of TA training.

During the 1970s, faculty development was a vehicle for bringing about change within institutions, especially as it related to the classroom. The focus of faculty development was improving instructional skills, often through workshops and seminars in areas such as course and curriculum design, teaching methodologies, interpersonal communication, and small group dynamics (Gaff and Justice 1978).

It has been estimated that in 1976 approximately half of American academic institutions had a faculty development program and that many of these programs were responsible for an increased interest in teaching, an awareness that improvement in teaching is possible, and an increase in evaluation of faculty (Gaff and Justice 1978).

During the 1980s, the underlying notion of faculty development changed from developing to revitalizing faculty, and the focus on instructional skills expanded to include concerns related to low faculty morale and the survival needs of academic institutions (Bland and Schmitz 1988). However, although the conceptualization of faculty development has expanded, the instructional development and teaching improvement components continue to exist on approximately half of American campuses, a figure that corresponds to that of 1976 (Erickson 1986).

The 1980s also were marked by a large and rapid increase in training programs for graduate teaching assistants. In fact, 90 percent of TA training programs were implemented during the last 10 years (Buerkel-Rothfuss and Gray 1991). A survey indicates that approximately 50 percent of academic departments that employ TAs offer some form of training and that 26 percent of colleges and universities offer campus-wide TA training that is separate from departmental programs (Buerkel-Rothfuss and Gray 1990). The purposes of TA training programs include improving the quality of undergraduate education and preparing TAs for their present TA responsibilities as well as their future roles as teaching faculty.

The content and design of TA training programs vary but often include course policies, classroom management, classroom climate, and instructional strategies (Weimer, Svinicki, and Bauer 1989). Common designs range from one-day to two-week orientations prior to the beginning of the term. Many programs also have periodic workshops during the term and use follow-up videotaping and/or peer observation of TA-taught classes. Some departments offer complete courses in the teaching of a specific subject. Cornell University, for example, offers a course on teaching writing that TAs take while they are teaching composition or working with a composition instructor (K. Gottschalk 1991).

In many ways, international teaching assistant training parallels TA training for native speakers of English: It includes classroom management, classroom climate, and instructional strategies (Weimer, Svinicki, and Bauer 1989). However, in important ways, it also differs from native-speaker TA training. The first difference is that English is not the native language of most ITAs. ITA training programs, therefore, need to assess the language proficiency of ITAs and, when needed, provide training to improve English proficiency, including pronunciation.

The second difference relates to the educational background of the ITAs. Most ITAs are natives of countries in which the education system differs from that of the United States. Such differing aspects often include philosophy and purpose, appropriate classroom behavior, and expected roles of teachers and students.

For example, in the PRC, the country with the highest number of graduate students in the United States, teachers are perceived as authorities in their fields and are expected to have mastered the content of their disciplines. One of the ways in which Chinese students demonstrate respect for their teachers is by refraining from asking questions. Students' questions are viewed as an insult to the teacher, and most teachers do not permit them (Hudson-Ross and Dong 1990).

In contrast, in the United States it is expected that students will ask questions, and it is appropriate for teachers to admit that they do not know an answer. Because of differences such as these, ITAs need instruction in American academic culture, specifically in those areas that undergraduates perceive as important to effective teaching and learning. When one considers that many ITAs eventually will move into faculty positions at American academic institutions, as noted earlier, ITA training becomes even more important.

Systems Analysis: Designing an Appropriate ITA Program

As universities have responded to the need for specialized training for ITAs, several program models have emerged. The literature clearly suggests that the selection or design of a TA or ITA program model be informed by research findings and an analysis of the structure, needs, resources, and context of a particular institution (Ard 1989; Constantinides 1987a; Ford et al. 1991; Sequeira and Costantino 1989; R. Smith, Byrd, Constantinides, and Barrett 1991; Smoch and Menges 1985; Weimer, Svinicki, and Bauer 1989).

An in-depth analysis of the institution as a system might include (1) study of the structure of U.S. research universities and their place in U.S. society, (2) study of the specific institution, (3) study of specific departments, and (4) study of the teaching styles and traditions of particular professions (R. Smith et al. 1991). Other methods of analyzing the institutional system appear in the literature in higher education administration (e.g., Kuh and Whitt 1988), ethnographic studies of higher education (e.g., Rounds 1985, 1987), and strategic planning literature (e.g., Bryson 1988).

These studies, based on analytical processes such as the culture audit (Kuh and Whitt 1988) and the environmental scan (Bryson 1988), provide rational bases for program design (R. Smith et al. 1991). An analysis of the university using these methods should reveal answers to the following questions, which are suggestive only of the multiplicity of factors that will affect the design of an ITA program:

- Why is the program being established?
- Which unit on campus can administer the program the most effectively?
- What institutional resources will be available to the program?
- How will the demographics of the student body affect the program?

Why is the program being established?

The motivating factors behind the program will influence its structure, including its goals and objectives. Programs developed because of a legislative mandate may be limited in scope to include just those issues and criteria named in the laws, generally the assessment of English language proficiency. For example, as previously discussed, 18 states man-

> *The motivating factors behind the program will influence its structure, including its goals and objectives.*

date assessment and/or training for ITAs and international faculty (Thomas and Monoson 1992). When this assessment must account for a mandated cut-off score on an examination, as it does in Florida, then the program designers must plan for the timely administration and scoring of the evaluation and must decide how to prepare prospective ITAs for the assessment.

If a program was developed, at least in part, to prevent legislative action, it may include a strong language assessment and development component as well as other curricular concerns. Such elements are intended to convince the legislators that no action on their part is required. An example is the University of Wyoming program (Constantinides 1987b).

Programs developed solely in response to a perceived need on campus may encompass the broadest curriculum and have goals that go beyond language assessment and development (Ford et al. 1991; R. Smith 1982).

Which unit on campus can administer the program the most effectively?

The importance of a systems analysis becomes clear in determining the most effective administrative location. For campus-wide programs to be successful, they must be housed in an administrative unit that has influence or authority across colleges and departments. Instructional development offices conduct some ITA programs; others are run by ESL departments or ESL teachers; still others are housed in individual departments, such as English, chemistry, or physics.

On many campuses, neither ESL nor instructional development is a politically powerful program nor does either have much visibility or influence within the institution (R. Smith et al. 1991). A campus-wide ITA program housed in an ESL program, for example, may have difficulty accomplishing its objectives unless the program has adequate support from the higher administration and a good working relationship with participating departments.

Generally, programs can function more effectively when administered by a unit that can give them appropriate credibility, funding, and authority (R. Smith et al. 1991). For objectives to be accomplished, programs must be designed around a realistic analysis of campus politics, the various interests served by the program (Ford et al. 1991), and the formal and informal power structures within the institution (R. Smith et al. 1991).

What institutional resources will be available to the program?

Another important variable affecting the design of the program is the availability of resources, including funding, faculty and staff, and facilities.

Funding. A large number of ITA programs began in the 1980s at a time when resources, while not abundant, were nevertheless more available than in the difficult financial times of the early 1990s. Even so, funding for ITA programs was, and continues to be, a difficult and politically sensitive issue on some campuses.

Byrd, R. Smith, and Constantinides (1990) studied the funding patterns at 43 universities in 1990. They found that ITA programs were funded with hard money (appropriated funds) and soft money (interest income, overhead, and fees, for example). Four of the programs surveyed were funded entirely from hard money, 14 entirely from soft money, 22 from a combination of hard and soft money, and three from unknown sources.

Of the 43 programs, only eight received all of their money from the same source (whether hard or soft money); 11 were funded from two sources; and 24 were funded from three or more sources. Some of the soft money was reported to be "funny" money—money, such as a tuition waiver, that is transferred from one account to another without ever appearing as real currency.

The cost for a one-semester three-credit training course and a one-semester oral skills class for approximately 40 to 50 ITAs is estimated to be at least $18,000. The estimated cost for a three-week intensive pre-term training program, including an oral skills component, for approximately 40 ITAs is at least $20,000 (Byrd, R. Smith, and Constantinides 1990).

The study revealed five different general categories of problems with funding: (1) insufficient funding to run the program adequately; (2) programs being operated in whole or in part with subsidies—without reimbursement from the institution; (3) inconsistent or ad hoc funding: no line-item budget, for example, or funding that must be sought every year from various sources; (4) programs needing expanded funding to enhance the program; and (5) miscellaneous problems, such as securing funding for stipends for a contract period for ITAs who fail the assessment and who cannot teach.

Clearly, the amount, source, and stability of the funding will affect program organization. During tight budgetary times, more and more institutions may adopt fee-based training—requiring that ITAs or international faculty pay for any necessary testing and training. For example, in Texas, a 1989 amendment to the Texas Education Code mandates that the cost of training programs or short courses be born by the faculty member and deducted from that person's salary (Texas Education Code). One response in Texas has been to offer training courses for credit and charge participants tuition for the training.

Faculty and staff. The availability of qualified faculty may affect program design. Whether a program is administered in an instructional development office, an ESL or intensive English program, or another academic department may depend, in part, on where the most qualified faculty and staff are located. Sometimes, individuals from different units on campus collaborate on a program. For example, from 1980 to 1987, the program at Texas Tech University included faculty and staff from ESL, the Department of Communication Studies, and the Office of International Programs (R. Smith 1982; R. Smith and Ainsworth 1987).

Facilities. Program directors also must consider the availability of space for testing and training programs. At many institutions, space-allocation priority goes to credit-granting programs (R. Smith et al. 1991). Since many ITA programs are not offered for credit, facilities may not be readily available even though the program may have a legal mandate. The facilities also should allow access to the equipment necessary to conduct the program, such as tape recorders, videocassette recorders, and other materials.

How will the demographics of the student body affect the program?

The demographics of the student body vary across regions and from institution to institution. The backgrounds of the students may affect their perceptions of the comprehensibility of ITAs. Greater listener familiarity with non-native speech in general, or with a specific non-native accent, facilitates the ability of native speakers to comprehend (Gass and Varonis 1984). Universities in metropolitan areas may attract students who have had more experience with linguistic and cultural diversity, whereas students from more rural or less cosmopolitan areas may have little or no experience with non-native English speakers in the classroom.

For example, a 1990 survey at the City College of the City University of New York revealed the ethnicity of the undergraduate respondents to be 39.2 percent black, 14.5 percent white, 0.4 percent American Indian/Alaskan Native, 5.9 percent Puerto Rican, 15.0 percent Hispanic, and 18.2 percent Asian-Pacific. At the same time, the ethnicity of 302 graduate teaching assistants in science (biology, chemistry/biochemistry, physics, engineering) was 47 percent Asian, 6.6 percent black, 5.6 percent Hispanic, and 40.7 percent "other." The researchers have noted that most of their undergraduate students are accustomed to hearing a diversity of accents and do not report this diversity to be a problem as much as do students in other geographical areas (Lay, Mantel, and Smiley 1991).

Fox studied the major concerns of stakeholders at a large Midwestern university with respect to the use of ITAs as instructors of undergraduates. Interviews with different groups of stakeholders, including undergraduates, revealed that more extensive difficulties with ITAs were perceived by undergraduate students than by the ITAs themselves or by administrators (1991). Thus, the extent to which the language skills and cultural differences of ITAs are perceived to be a problem might well affect the goals and structure of the curriculum of the program.

Other demographic factors, such as high school background and average age of the undergraduates, can affect the undergraduate students' general maturity and preparedness for university work and openness to having an ITA as an instructor.

The systems analysis, then, can provide a clearer understanding of the institution—its structure, its students, its resources, and its constituencies; such understanding is critical to the design and establishment of an effective program (R. Smith et al. 1991).

ITA Program Designs

Because of the diversity in types of programs, it is difficult to develop a typology that fits every individual circumstance.

However, many programs appear to be based on the typology that categorizes programs as orientation, pre-term (also called pre-term/pre-teach), or concurrent (Constantinides 1987a; R. Smith et al. 1991). These models are a combination of the design elements, which focus on the timing and framework of the program, and the curricular components. The designs vary in length, timing, cost, credit-basis, and logistical complexity. The effect of these areas on program content will be discussed under curricular issues.

Orientation program designs

The general purpose of an orientation is to familiarize participants with the campus, institutional policies, and campus resources. In the case of ITAs, the orientation also may serve to inform them about cultural differences and perhaps provide some language or other training. Orientation programs typically take place either immediately before the beginning of a term (pre-term) or during the term (concurrent) and last from six to 40 hours, or the equivalent of one to five days (Constantinides 1987a; R. Smith et al. 1991).

Pre-term orientation programs. Pre-term orientation programs sometimes serve only ITAs. In other situations, they are part of a general orientation for all new TAs, including native English speakers (Constantinides 1987a; R. Smith et al. 1991; Weimer, Svinicki, and Bauer 1989). Mississippi State University, for example, has a seven-day orientation; the first two days are for TAs/ITAs, whereas the final five days are only for ITAs (Lyons 1989). The five-day intensive orientation program at the University of Illinois at Urbana-Champaign has incorporated collegial sharing, cross-cultural classroom issues, and practice mini-lessons to build communicative competence (Hahn 1989).

Pre-term orientation programs have several advantages. They may be less expensive than longer programs because neither stipends for the participants nor special housing arrangements normally are required. If the programs are piggybacked onto a general orientation for international students or all new TAs, the cost is reduced and the logistics of the orientation program become easier to arrange. Although time is somewhat limited, careful selection of materials can provide basic survival information for the new ITAs. Since the new ITAs are not yet teaching or taking classes, they may be more free to concentrate on the orientation, especially if they already have been attending the institution (Constantinides 1987a; R. Smith et al. 1991).

However, the timing of the orientation model near the beginning of the term also could serve as a disadvantage. ITAs who are newly arrived from overseas or from out of town often are very busy meeting their advisors, registering for classes, opening bank accounts, finding housing, and other tasks. The new ITAs also must begin to prepare to teach their classes. These demands on the ITAs' time may detract from the effectiveness of the orientation program. An additional problem is that if an orientation program attempts to present too much information in such a short period of time, the ITAs may be unable to process or assimilate it (Constantinides 1987a; R. Smith et al. 1991).

In addition to considerations of settling in, ITAs who are newly arrived may not have their ears attuned to American English or unfamiliar regional accents. If new ITAs arrive with pronunciation or other language problems, a brief orientation program may not afford them enough time to make any lasting changes in pronunciation or become comfortable with their listening skills.

An orientation program also may not provide time for activities that other program designs often build into their curriculum, such as videotaping, teaching simulations, or meaningful practice with presentation skills (see discussion of curricular components). In addition, credit classes are not in session at this time, so new ITAs are unable to observe what actually occurs in an American classroom in terms of student-teacher interactions and behaviors (Constantinides 1987a; R. Smith et al. 1991).

Pre-term orientation with follow-up. A variation of the pre-term orientation model is an orientation with a follow-up during the term that may include group meetings, consultations with advisors or ITA training faculty, videotaping, and other activities. If this type of follow-up occurs, it may add to the cost of the program, depending on the specific activities and personnel involved (Constantinides 1987a).

A proposal for a program at the City College of the City University of New York included a two-day orientation for ITAs followed by a three-day workshop for TAs and ITAs; fall follow-up activities also were suggested (Mantel 1989). The

University of Nevada-Reno has used a two-day August orientation with follow-up group seminars in the fall (Johncock 1987b).

Concurrent orientation. An orientation program that takes place during the ITAs' first term in the classroom is referred to as concurrent, because it occurs during the term rather than immediately preceding it. Concurrent orientation programs limit instruction and training to approximately six to 40 hours—significantly fewer than those in the pre-teach/pre-term model discussed later. Additional activities, such as those included in the follow-up to the pre-term orientation, may complement the basic orientation to the university.

The concurrent orientation can be scheduled so it lengthens the amount of time ITAs have to assimilate the information presented in the program. Another advantage is that classes are available for the ITAs to observe.

However, because a concurrent orientation program takes place during the ITAs' first term teaching, it has several disadvantages. Since the ITAs would have teaching duties during this first term, they probably would not have had adequate preparation and training for their teaching responsibilities. Additionally, since orientation programs ordinarily are not credit-bearing, most ITAs will be enrolled in a full load of courses—nine to 15 hours, depending on the department— and teaching one to two courses. In this case, the ITAs may be reluctant to spend time on an activity for which they receive no credit (R. Smith et al. 1991).

Pre-term/pre-teach program designs
Pre-term/pre-teach program. The second type of program design is the pre-term model (Constantinides 1987a), also called the pre-term/pre-teach model (R. Smith et al. 1991). Pre-term/pre-teach programs occur in the summer before the fall term begins and before the participants meet their first class. These programs generally include instruction in language, pedagogy, and culture and provide numerous opportunities for the ITAs to practice their presentation skills.

Pre-term programs may or may not have any credit attached. The length of the pre-term program varies from a minimum of about two weeks to up to eight weeks, although two to four weeks is probably the most common. Examples include the University of Delaware, with a four-week program (Schneider

TABLE 4

ORIENTATION PROGRAMS

A. Pre-term Orientation

Length	1-5 days
Content	1. survival information and orientation to the institution and its setting
	2. some language, culture and pedagogy
Credit/non-credit	both
Advantages	1. comparatively low cost
	2. comparatively simple logistics
	3. comparatively few competing demands
Disadvantages	1. registration week distractions
	2. cognitive overload
	3. no time to adjust to American accent
	4. insufficient time for changes in language
	5. little time to practice skills
	6. little instruction in pedagogy
	7. little instruction in language skills
	8. no classes to observe

B. Pre-term Orientation with Follow-Up

Length of follow-up	varies
Content of follow-up	varies, may include videotaping for individual critiques, group meetings, retreats
Credit/non-credit for the follow-up	non-credit
Advantages	1. lengthens time available to assimilate material
	2. can include some instruction on pedagogy
Disadvantages	may add to cost

C. Concurrent Orientation

Length	6-40 hours
Content	1. some survival information and orientation to the institution and its setting
	2. language, culture, and pedagogy
Advantages	1. more time to assimilate information
	2. can include greater variety of material
Disadvantages	1. no training before teaching
	2. may be more costly than pre-term orientation
	3. distractions of other duties and classes prevent full participation by ITAs

and Stevens 1987), and the University of Missouri-Columbia, with a two-and-a-half-week design (vom Saal, Miles, and McGraw 1988).

There are a number of advantages associated with this model related to the length of time the ITAs spend in the program. Most pre-term programs last from four to six hours a day and provide the ITAs with an intensive training experience. ITAs have the opportunity to be videotaped while they present brief talks to practice various presentation styles, work on listening comprehension and selected aspects of their pronunciation and other language skills, and become accustomed to the university environment. More time also is available for the instructors to assess the ITAs' ability in a variety of communicative contexts. Since the ITAs are not teaching, taking classes, registering, or going through other orientation programs simultaneously, they can devote their time and energy to the training program (Constantinides 1987a; R. Smith et al. 1991).

A significant advantage to the pre-term model is the opportunity the ITAs have to prepare themselves for the all-important first day of classes (Constantinides 1987a). Wolcowitz asserts that the first day of class very well may determine the tone of the class for the balance of the term, since that is when teachers and students negotiate, in a sense, what will happen during the class (Wolcowitz 1982).

Just as the additional length of the pre-term model is an advantage, it also presents significant disadvantages. First and foremost are the funding and logistical problems. In some programs, ITAs receive a stipend in the form of a salary, housing, or food. For example, Texas Tech University provides on-campus housing and food for ITAs coming in from out of town to attend the program (R. Smith 1982; R. Smith and Ainsworth 1987). The University of Wyoming provides housing and food stipends to its participants (Constantinides 1987a). Other institutions, including the University of Delaware (Schneider and Stevens 1987), pay their ITAs a regular stipend for attending their intensive summer training programs.

Additional program costs relate to teaching staff, clerical and technical support, and equipment. Other logistical problems during a pre-term program may be a lack or shortage of campus housing or food service and the availability of qualified staff during the summer.

Some academic departments and deans may oppose a pre-term model, believing that it will hurt their recruiting program because some ITAs are reluctant to arrive early for a training program (Constantinides 1987a). Summer school classes may or may not overlap with the workshop, and it may not be possible for the ITAs to observe classes, since these programs usually occur in August.

In some programs, undergraduate students play an important role in the assessment of ITAs (Plakans and Abraham 1990; Schneider and Stevens 1991). In the micro-teaching practice sessions, undergraduate students sometimes serve as authentic "class" members or tutors (Ford et al. 1991).

In a pre-term model, it may be more difficult to find undergraduate students who are willing or available to participate in the program during a pre-term session.

If the institution has a large number of new ITAs, the preterm model may prove to be difficult to coordinate and may involve additional cost if a number of sections of courses are required.

Pre-term/pre-teach with follow-up. A variation of the preterm model involves a pre-term session with a follow-up course or follow-up activities during the regular term. This model is used, for example, at Texas Tech University (R. Smith and Ainsworth 1987) and the University of Wyoming (Constantinides 1987a). During the follow-up course, ITAs may have group meetings and may be observed in their classroom. They also may receive the opportunity that was missing from the pre-term program to observe other undergraduate classes. A follow-up course allows trainers to monitor the ITAs during their first term teaching and to intervene or provide support and assistance, if necessary, before major problems arise in the classroom.

The University of Nebraska-Lincoln offers several follow-up options to ITAs. Depending on their individual needs, ITAs who do not successfully complete the pre-term training program may take ESL workshops or college teaching seminars or may repeat the ITA workshop. The follow-up for ITAs who are successful and hold teaching assignments includes classroom observation, feedback sessions, and surveys. Optional monthly noon-time discussion sessions are available for all TAs, including ITAs (Ford et al. 1991).

TABLE 5

PRE-TERM/PRE-TEACH PROGRAMS

A. Pre-term/Pre-teach Programs

Length	2-8 weeks
Content	language, pedagogy, culture, practice
Credit/non-credit	both
Advantages	1. intensive training
	2. time for extensive evaluation
	3. few distractions
	4. opportunities to practice presentation skills
	5. time to attune ear and improve listening comprehension
Disadvantages	1. higher cost than orientation program
	2. logistically difficult (housing, staff)
	3. few or no classes to observe
	4. no follow-up

B. Pre-term/Pre-teach Program with Follow-up

Length of follow-up	term-long
Content of follow-up	reinforcement and observation
Credit/non-credit for follow-up	both
Advantages	1. provides follow-up to summer training
	2. opportunities for ITAs to observe classes
Disadvantages	higher cost than orientation program

Term-long concurrent program designs

A program is concurrent if it takes place during the regular academic term rather than during the break between the summer and fall terms. A term-long concurrent program is different from a concurrent orientation in terms of the type and amount of material presented and the number of hours of instruction in the course. The concurrent orientation focuses more on immediate instructional needs and administrative issues and usually ranges from six to 40 hours. Concurrent programs, on the other hand, may occur during the ITA's first term teaching or prior to the ITA's teaching (concurrent pre-teach). The content is often very similar to that of a pre-term program. Some concurrent programs are offered for credit; others are non-credit. Concurrent programs generally are scheduled for the equivalent of three hours a week, although Pennsylvania State University, for example, offers or has offered 10-hour per week training sessions (Dunkel and Rahman 1987).

Term-long concurrent program/pre-teach. The pre-teach term-long concurrent program takes place before the ITA assumes classroom teaching responsibilities.

Since pre-teach term-long concurrent programs occur during the regular term, no special housing costs or supplementary summer stipends are associated with them. In some cases, the training staff already is on contract and does not require supplemental salaries. Clerical support sometimes is contributed by the administrative unit in which the program is housed. In short, not as much extra cost for housing and staff is associated with concurrent programs as with pre-term programs (Constantinides 1987a).

Another advantage to this design is associated with the fact that the time the ITAs are in the training program is scheduled over a 10- to 15-week term. ITAs have time to work on their pronunciation and other language skills, develop their listening comprehension, observe classes, and assimilate the wealth of material that is included in many programs. Additionally, the pre-teach concurrent program does not place ITAs in the classroom for at least one term; therefore, it is possible to evaluate thoroughly that ITA's readiness for classroom duties.

The primary disadvantage of the pre-teach concurrent program is the associated cost. Departments must pay their ITAs whether or not they perform teaching duties. Departments may not have enough funds to pay these ITAs during the training program and still hire additional instructors to cover the classes that these ITAs would have been teaching (Constantinides 1987a).

Also, the concurrent program may not be advisable for an institution that must use all of its TAs and ITAs to teach during the first term. It would be difficult—if not impossible—to conduct appropriate pre-teaching assessment and training (R. Smith et al. 1991).

Term-long concurrent programs/while teaching. If the training occurs at the same time the ITA is teaching, the program is called "term-long concurrent program/while teaching" training. Such programs generally occur during an ITA's first term in an instructional setting.

In a concurrent/while teaching program, the ITAs can more easily recognize the need for their training since they are in a classroom setting. They can try new techniques and discuss

Not as much extra cost for housing and staff is associated with concurrent programs as with pre-term programs.

immediate problems with others in the program.

However, ITAs who are teaching while taking the course may not be ready for classroom responsibilities. In this scenario, ITAs already have met their first class before they have any preparation and already may have made an irreparably bad impression on their students (Constantinides 1987a). If ITAs are taking a concurrent program for no credit, they may be reluctant to spend time on it instead of on their "real" classes.

New TAs, especially, often are surprised by how much time it takes to perform as a TA and a full-time student. Some must take the training program with no reduction in their course load in their department. These ITAs often resent the time required to prepare for a training program, which they sometimes see as an unimportant burden (Constantinides 1987a).

Many different uses and combinations of these models are possible, depending on the number of ITAs in the program,

TABLE 6

CONCURRENT PROGRAMS

A. Pre-teach Concurrent Programs

Length	10-16 weeks
Content	language, culture, pedagogy, practice
Credit/non-credit	both
Advantages	1. ample time for training before teaching
	2. time to effect change in pronunciation
	3. time for listening comprehension to improve
	4. classes are available for ITAs to observe
	5. more time for ITAs to assimilate information
Disadvantages	1. higher cost to university
	2. ITAs may have negative attitude toward extra class

B. Concurrent Programs While Teaching

Length	10-16 weeks
Content	language, pedagogy, culture, practice
Credit/non-credit	both
Advantages	ITAs can relate training to the here and now
Disadvantages	1. ITAs must teach before and during training
	2. ITAs may begin semester making a bad impression on students

the availability and expertise of the staff, the type and amount of support services, and the availability of funding. Pennsylvania State University has had a sequence of three courses for ITAs, including speaking and listening, teaching methodology, and culture (Dunkel and Rahman 1987). Some universities have employed several of these models over time as their programs developed and responded to institutional needs. For example, the University of Wyoming used a concurrent model from 1982-85 and in 1986 changed to a preterm program plus follow-up model (Constantinides 1987a).

Other institutions use combinations of the orientation or pre-term models with concurrent models. For example, at the University of Washington, ITAs attend a one-week preterm workshop followed by two quarters of seminars and tutorials (Sequeira and Darling 1987). Michigan State University offers a two-week pre-term orientation program with the possibility of a 10-week ITA program and/or a 10-week language training program (Lyons 1989).

At the University of Michigan, ITAs attend three-week summer intensive workshop courses on pedagogy, culture, and language. Follow-up class observation and consultation services are available throughout the year, and the English Language Institute offers five additional specialized courses for ITAs (Morley 1991).

L. Lambert and Tice (1993) have compiled 72 detailed profiles of TA and ITA training programs—centralized and discipline-based—as well as a program directory that provides contact names, addresses, and telephone numbers for more than 350 additional programs.

Curricular Components
The second component of an ITA program model is the curriculum, the structure of which will be informed by the results of the systems analysis and the program design chosen. The curriculum design must address at least the following questions:
- What skills does a successful teaching assistant need?
- What topics should be included in the program that will help the teaching assistant acquire these skills?

What skills does a successful teaching assistant need?
The literature on teaching suggests that effective teachers should have subject matter competency, good presentation

skills, and good human relations skills (Eble 1983; Lowman 1984; McKeachie 1978). Seventeen studies related to specific teaching skills that are useful for ITAs are discussed in the research section of this report. The skills range from being friendly and interactive to asking students questions to using the blackboard in an organized manner.

Clearly, the specific skills needed by an ITA also vary depending on the tasks the ITA must perform in the instructional setting (Young 1990). For example, the needs of ITAs who work as laboratory instructors (Myers and Douglas 1991; Myers and Plakans 1990, 1991), discussion group leaders, or lecturers are directly related to their teaching assignments.

What topics should be included in the program that will help the teaching assistant acquire these skills?

Most pre-term/pre-teach and concurrent programs include four primary topics in the curriculum: (1) language, (2) pedagogy, (3) culture, and (4) micro-teaching practice. These four topics affect presentation and human relations skills. However, subject-matter competency usually is not included in college or campus-wide programs, since such competency is assumed to be a departmental matter.

A curriculum that includes language, pedagogy, culture, and practice may more easily address all of the communicative competence needs of the ITAs. Such a curriculum would reflect the roles of the ITAs as instructors of U.S. undergraduates instead of primarily focusing on language. Communicative competence needs include the ITAs' ability to (1) use the language grammatically and comprehensibly, (2) function in various culturally influenced communicative contexts, including the classroom, (3) produce and interpret discourse coherently, and (4) utilize strategies to compensate for weaknesses in the other three areas (Hoekje and Williams 1992).

Language. As previously mentioned, when national and educationally related press coverage about the "ITA problem" appeared in the 1980s, that problem most often was perceived to be based on poor English skills, especially pronunciation. Among the most difficult tasks for the ITA program director is to determine (1) to what extent pronunciation is a problem for each ITA, (2) how to assess pronunciation objectively, (3) what the threshold level of pronunciation is below which comprehensible instruction cannot take place, and (4) how to help ITAs improve their pronunciation. Six studies related to undergraduates' perceptions of the pronunciation of ITAs are reviewed in the section in this text on research; the assessment of pronunciation and other language skills is addressed in some detail in the following section on assessment.

The teaching of pronunciation in ITA courses takes various forms. For example, the use of drama may improve ITAs' pronunciation (Stevens 1989). Wennerstrom developed pronunciation materials with tasks that range in complexity from controlled to semi-controlled to free; these tasks encourage the transfer of skills from practice activities to free speech in the teaching environment (1989a). Some programs include computer-assisted instruction for accent reduction (e.g., Johnson, Dunkel, and Rekart 1991; Stenson, Downing, J. Smith, and K. Smith 1991). Bolivar and Sarwark produce individualized audiotaped tutorials about ITAs' videotaped presentations; the audiotapes contain key terms and phrases mispronounced by the ITA and suggest drills (1990).

Other studies indicate that language training, especially short-term training, should focus primarily on stress, rhythm, and intonation, rather than on individual sounds (Acton, Gilbert, and Wong 1987; Anderson-Hsieh 1990). Individualized instruction for language skills also may be advantageous (Constantinides 1987a). Working with prospective ITAs on the pronunciation of key terms or key phrases in their discipline may produce better results in the classroom than trying to focus on discrete sounds in a short period of time (Byrd, Hurt, and Constantinides 1988). Additional language practice and a focus on field-specific language also are suggested ways to enhance ITA curricula (J. Smith 1992).

Pronunciation is not the only aspect of language that must be considered. ITAs should be skilled at reading aloud in their discipline, since they often have to read problems, announcements, test questions, and other information to students. ITAs also should possess acceptable grammatical skills—both oral and written. Some grammatical problems that afflict many ITAs, such as the improper use of the definite article, can quickly become irritating to students. Good writing skills also are important for preparing tests and syllabi.

Whatever the specific goals and objectives of the language component of the curriculum, these goals and objectives should be consistent with the overall goals of the program and attainable within the program design. For example, one might expect better results in pronunciation over the course of a full term than over a two- or three-week period. It is unlikely, therefore, that one would have global changes in pronunciation as a goal for a pre-term program (R. Smith et al. 1991).

Pedagogy. It appears reasonably clear from research that undergraduates favor instructors who exhibit certain behaviors such as providing feedback, making eye contact, inviting comments and questions, and so forth. The importance of ITAs' using "teacher talk" that includes an interactive style and the appropriate use of discourse markers is noted as well (Inglis and Dalle 1992).

Questions remain, however, about the issue of teaching styles and good teaching in the design and conduct of the training program itself (Byrd and Constantinides 1988). If a training program is to be perceived as being effective by academic departments, ITA trainers in centralized programs must be able to extend beyond the preferred style of their own discipline and present teaching styles that are appropriate to a variety of classroom settings (Byrd 1987a; Byrd and Constantinides 1988; R. Smith et al. 1991). At Columbia University, for example, the ITA program uses a professional education perspective intended to develop both presentation skills and professional attitudes and values (Boyd 1989).

Other pedagogical issues include identifying teaching styles, strategies, and traditions that are appropriate not just to the discipline but also to the institution; teaching ITAs strategies for interaction with students in and out of the classroom; teaching ITAs how to repair communication when it breaks down; and discussing a variety of direct and indirect questioning techniques. Additional topics might cover issues of fairness and equity in the classroom, test preparation and grading, and the effective use of audiovisual equipment. Axelson and Madden (1990) describe the interactive use of video and discuss some of the issues that must be considered in designing video-based tasks.

Culture. Many of the pedagogical issues discussed here also must be looked at in the light of cultural differences. Culture must be defined broadly to include institutional culture, disciplinary sub-cultures, and classroom culture (Sadow and Maxwell 1983; R. Smith 1989; R. Smith et al. 1991). ITAs also should be made aware of the cultural expectations and attitudes of the American undergraduate students whom they will teach. It has been suggested that ITAs should learn about the characteristics of the U.S. educational system and the behavioral norms of classrooms in the United States (Bernhardt 1987). It has been proposed that ITAs consider switching cultural roles as well as languages in order to teach successfully in a foreign university (Pialorsi 1984). "The ability to assume a culturally alien persona is an important part of what we mean by capacity for language or overall communicative competence" (pp. 17-18).

The attitudes of ITAs toward their students, the ITAs' demeanor in front of a class, how the ITAs handle before- and after-class time, their attitudes toward questions, and their attitudes toward women and minorities in the class (Graham 1992) will contribute to their effectiveness in the classroom. ITA trainers should have sufficient contact with undergraduate students to be able to provide accurate information in this regard (R. Smith et al. 1991). Classroom observation is especially helpful in accomplishing these goals, since the ITAs can observe how undergraduates interact with American teachers and other students and how teachers conduct themselves in class. Davies and Tyler describe a research/teaching methodology that discovers the sources of miscommunication between ITAs and undergraduates and makes the sources explicit to participants so cross-linguistic and cross-cultural differences can be examined (1989).

Micro-teaching practice. The final curricular aspect that most programs include is that of a practicum or practice component that consists of micro-teaching experiences. These provide the participants with an opportunity to integrate some of the individual topics and skills presented in the program. Typically, the ITA will present a lecture of five to 10 minutes defining, for example, a term from his or her field or describing a process.

Evaluations of ITA programs as well as anecdotal reports suggest that one aspect of programs that participants find most helpful is that of being able to practice giving talks in their field and receiving feedback. A popular approach to the practice component is videotaped micro-teaching. For example, in the program at Texas Tech University, ITAs are videotaped a minimum of three times during the pre-term training program (R. Smith and Ainsworth 1987). While other programs may offer different numbers of videotaped presentations, many include some type of videotaping of ITAs micro-teaching or performing other practice activities. Other teaching practice builds on non-videotaped teaching simulations and leading discussions.

Other curricular issues. Besides the four basic curricular components, programs may include additional topics such as laboratory safety, sexual harassment, and diversity in the classroom. ITA trainers at Drexel University and the University of Pennsylvania, for example, recommend including safety issues and safety communication concerns in the ITA program. The language skills identified include comprehension of safety requirements, oral language and pedagogical skills necessary to teach and enforce lab safety, and oral English skills needed to respond to lab emergencies (Barnes and van Naerssen 1991). Other issues include ensuring that ITAs understand their legal rights and responsibilities with regard to lab safety, and the importance of not taking shortcuts that could result in laboratory accidents (Barnes and van Naerssen 1991).

Graham reports on the inclusion of instruction on bias-free teaching in an ITA course (1992). In 1991, the program at Texas Tech University began to include a session focusing on sexual harassment and gender bias in the classroom. A related topic is how ITAs may respond to ethnic diversity in the classroom in terms of stereotyping and grading practices (S. Jenkins and Rubin 1991).

Implementation Issues

The models described thus far are a combination of program design and curricular components. However, other programmatic issues also must be considered, such as procedures for notification of ITAs, a process for screening ITAs' language abilities, exit evaluations, enforcement, (Constantinides 1987a), and texts and materials. Screening processes and exit evaluations will be considered in a following section.

Notification

ITAs who are required to arrive on campus early for a program must have timely notification so the requirements of the Immigration and Naturalization Service can be met and travel arrangements made. Prospective ITAs already residing in the

United States or on campus need to be identified. This process depends on cooperation between the program director, the academic department, and the admissions office (Constantinides 1987a).

Enforcement. Enforcement issues are critical to the success of a program. State-mandated testing and training programs can be enforced by law. However, non-legislatively mandated programs sometimes are required by the institution, while in other cases the programs are optional. Some institutions with required programs, such as Texas Tech University and the University of Wyoming, strictly enforce the outcome of the screening and training process. If an ITA does not successfully complete the assessment or training, the ITA either cannot teach or must take additional training concurrent with his or her teaching (Constantinides 1987a; R. Smith and Ainsworth 1987). However, awkward situations may occur when some departments within the institution require their ITAs to attend a program, and others do not consider it mandatory (Ford et al. 1991). Other institutions may regard the outcome as purely advisory and leave the final decision to the ITA's academic department.

Texts and materials

Three ITA training texts are available through major publishers: *The Foreign Teaching Assistant's Manual* (Byrd, Constantinides, and Pennington 1989), *Teaching Matters: Skills and Strategies for International Teaching Assistants* (Pica, Barnes, and Finger 1990), and *Communicate: Strategies for International Teaching Assistants* (J. Smith, Meyers, and Burkhalter 1992). The manner in which the texts might be used in a program depends, to a large extent, on the goals and design of the program. All three texts offer commentary and exercises in pedagogy and culture in the classroom. Byrd, Constantinides, and Pennington (1989) and J. Smith, Meyers, and Burkhalter (1992) also include explanations and exercises on various aspects of English pronunciation, stress, and intonation.

As mentioned, the 1990 annotated bibliography (Briggs et al. 1990) lists some of the texts, materials, and videotapes that have been produced for ITA training, including, for example, Althen (1988); Boyd, Lane, and Merdinger (1989); Douglas and Myers (1987); Gunesekera and Swales (1987); Mellor (1988); Ronkowski, with McMurtrey, Zhuang, and

Myers (1986); Swales and Rounds (1985); and Wennerstrom (1989b). Briggs et al. (1990) provide a brief synopsis of the materials as well as some commentary. Other university-produced materials include, for example, Cohen and Robin (1985) and Gburek and Dunnett (1986). Although these materials are not available through major commercial publishers, some can be obtained by contacting the authors or the institutions that produced them; others may be available through the ERIC Clearinghouse.

Programs for International Faculty

Although numerous ITA programs exist across the country, almost no organized courses are designed exclusively for tenured or tenure-track international faculty. On campuses with centralized instructional development offices, international faculty may participate in programs with other faculty. In states like Texas, where assessment and training are mandated for all faculty whose primary language is not English, some institutions have individualized training programs or programs drawn up on an ad hoc basis.

At the University of Washington, international faculty may work on a consulting basis with the Center for Instructional Development and Research. The consultant works with the faculty member to identify problems and issues; collect, analyze, and interpret data; and finally, to translate the data into a set of recommendations and goals (Sequeira 1990). At the University of Michigan, international faculty may participate in tutorials through the English Language Institute (ELI) Speaking Clinic services. These international faculty tutorials, which began in 1987, may be either one-on-one or small group and include extensive videotaping and critiques (*English Language Institute* 1991). In addition to the tutorials, the Center for Research on Learning and Teaching (CRLT) offers evening courses for all faculty in areas such as organizing and presenting lectures, conducting discussions, and public speaking skills. The ELI and the CRLT are working to implement special sections of these courses for international faculty (Joan Morley, June 19, 1992, personal communication).

The program models, curricular components, and implementation issues discussed previously are constantly being tested and refined by program directors and researchers across the country. ITA trainers depend on a systems analysis to clarify the structure of their institutions and look to research findings to inform the design and instructional decisions that they must make. Research and systems analysis also can assist program directors with selecting or developing an appropriate system of assessment and integrating it into the overall program design.

ASSESSMENT ISSUES IN ITA TRAINING

The assessment of the teaching performed by teaching assistants in general and the evaluation of the English language capabilities of ITAs have been a matter of long-standing concern in U.S. higher education. In a close examination of official reports from Michigan State University, the University of California at Berkeley, and Cornell University, all of which dealt with the improvement of undergraduate teaching during the mid-1960s, Chase cited the various recommendations regarding the situation of TAs, including ITAs (1970). In each of these reports, specific recommendations were made regarding the need for better evaluation of TA teaching. In two of the three, recommendations called for improvements in the screening of ITAs with respect to their spoken English ability (Chase 1970). Twenty-five years later, these problems are still with us, especially the issue of ITA screening (Heller 1985, 1986).

For the majority of American TAs now teaching in large U.S. research universities, the means of assessing their work has not changed noticeably.

Assessment of TAs as a Context for ITA Assessment

Assessment in some form probably has been an integral part of the general use of graduate students as teaching assistants since its beginning in U.S. higher education. Very likely, the first TAs were required to submit to the same system of instructional evaluation as were their seniors on the faculty; this probably took the form of end-of-term questionnaires completed by the undergraduate students. Close observation of most TA-taught classes by selected members of the faculty, at least at first, no doubt provided additional evaluative information for assessment purposes.

Today, the literature suggests that for the majority of American TAs now teaching in large U.S. research universities, the means of assessing their work has not changed noticeably. External evaluations, in the form of end-of-term course evaluations and observational visits by members of the TA's department, are two of the most common types of assessment (Allen and Rueter 1990; Bort and Buerkel-Rothfuss 1991b; Pica, Barnes, and Finger 1990). However, Andrews (1987a, 1987b) and Lawrence (1987) have pointed out a great need for consistent and even-handed application of the assessment tools in use today in U.S. higher education as a whole, as well as within specific universities.

Other forms of external assessment include peer evaluation from other TAs and observations by staff from institutional faculty development centers (Franck and DeSousa 1982; Landa

1988; Pica, Barnes, and Finger 1990). The literature suggests that structured self-evaluation, especially that conducted by the observation of videotaped TA classes, has become an important form of TA assessment (Allen and Rueter 1990; Boehrer 1987; Pica, Barnes, and Finger 1990). Seventy-two percent of the nearly 1,400 TAs and ITAs surveyed at eight major research universities requested training in self-evaluation techniques (R.M. Diamond and P.J. Gray 1987).

The evaluation of ITAs in recent years has brought a new level of complexity to TA assessment, as shown by a variety of descriptive, analytical, and research studies appearing in the 1980s and early 1990s (a few examples include K. Bailey 1982; Barnes 1990; Davey and Marion 1987; Dege 1983; Gillespie 1988; Inglis 1988; Rounds 1987). Finally, the evaluation of training programs for TAs and ITAs appears as an increasingly important area for research in the literature on TA assessment (Bort and Buerkel-Rothfuss 1991a, 1991b; B. Davis 1987; Stevens 1988).

The term "assessment" as used herein will have various meanings, depending on the context of the discussion. It is meant to comprehend all forms of evaluative information, both quantitative and qualitative, including student/class questionnaires and surveys, observations of teaching by faculty and peers, supervisor end-of-term evaluations, various forms of self-evaluation, and standardized tests and other evaluative instruments used to assess TA teaching performance and ITA English language ability, teaching performance, and cross-cultural awareness.

Evaluation of TA performance
There are three types of formal assessment of TA teaching: instructional rating forms completed by the TA's students, usually at the end of the term; in-class observational visits by the TA's supervisor, staff from the institution's instructional development center, or faculty members from the department in which the TA is teaching; and end-of-term overall evaluations completed by the TA's supervisor or the department chair. Other types of assessment, often less formal, are evaluations performed by the TA's peers and self-evaluation.

End-of-term student instructional ratings. Buerkel-Rothfuss and P.L. Gray report that more than 75 percent of the 339 departments responding to their national survey of graduate teaching assistant training used a student instructional rating (SIR) form to assess the teaching effectiveness of TAs (1990). The SIR form usually is completed by the TA's students at term end, although other less formal means of gathering useful feedback from students earlier in the term recently have been promoted in the literature (Allen and Rueter 1990; Duba-Biedermann 1991).

Bort and Buerkel-Rothfuss analyzed the content of 65 evaluation forms and 25 other assessment procedures from U.S. universities (such as in-class observations and end-of-term TA assessments by supervisors) and categorized the teaching skills and behavioral features assessed therein (1991b). They found 102 separate evaluation items, such as the instructor's ability to "explain abstract concepts" and his or her "promptness in returning homework." They also found ten "dimensions" of TA evaluation items: professionalism, facilitation skills, interpersonal skills, presentation skills, preparation, student feedback, evaluation skills, application skills, knowledge, and accessibility.

In-class observations. Another very common type of TA assessment is the in-class observational visit to the TA's class. These visits are conducted by the TA's course director, supervisor, mentor, peer evaluator, or other department faculty, usually with a follow-up consultation with the TA. In the Buerkel-Rothfuss and P.L. Gray survey, more than 50 percent of the responding departments indicated that in-class visitations were used for general TA assessment (1990). Bort and Buerkel-Rothfuss note that while 37 of the same evaluation items are evaluated by the SIR forms and in-class observations, the SIR forms covered 50 additional evaluation items not included in the in-class observational measures (1991b; see preceding paragraph). In-class measures dealt almost exclusively with facilitation skills, interpersonal skills, presentation skills, and preparation—those areas of teaching that are easily assessed by direct observation (Pons 1987; Taylor 1987).

End-of-term evaluations by TA supervisor. Many departments depend on end-of-term evaluations of TA teaching prepared by the TA's supervisor, course director, mentor, or department chair (Henke 1987). Bort and Buerkel-Rothfuss note that the supervisor's evaluations in their sample centered mainly on the dimensions of professionalism and student feedback with only one or two evaluation items from the dimensions of application skills, knowledge, and accessibility (1991b).

They point out that a discrepancy exists between the areas assessed in the class observational visits and those assessed by the supervisor's end-of-term evaluation and the SIR measures. They suggest that an outstanding weakness of the TA assessment system is the possibility that TAs do not receive adequate information from the faculty who have made visits to their classes. Such information might include TAs' performance on professionalism evaluation items, such as dependability, initiative, punctuality, cooperation, flexibility, open-mindedness, and the ability to accept criticism of his or her ideas. If warned in time about "unprofessional" teaching behaviors, the TAs might be able to make correctional changes by term's end to avoid their supervisors' unfavorable end-of-term evaluation. The authors conclude that the in-class visitation measure should include many more of the professionalism evaluation items upon which the supervisors' end-of-term evaluations are based (Bort and Buerkel-Rothfuss 1991b).

Peer evaluation. In most cases, the literature suggests that peer evaluation of a TA's teaching by fellow TAs is a means to the TA's development as a teacher rather than a formal assessment measure used by the TA's department (Allen and Rueter 1990; Pica, Barnes, and Finger 1990). Peer evaluation is often a feature of TA training programs when used with micro-teaching exercises (Franck and DeSousa 1982; Landa 1988; P. Lee 1987; Mestenhauser, Perry, Paige, Landa, Brutsch, Dege, Doyle, Gillette, Hughes, Judy, Keye, Murphy, J. Smith, Vandersluis, and Wendt 1980). The literature shows that in some institutions and training programs, peer evaluations are well-structured and use organized report forms and feedback systems; others are very informal and unstructured, existing only as a vague "requirement" of the TA training program (Stelzner 1987).

There appear to be numerous advantages to the peer form of assessment. A class observation by a peer tends to be less threatening to the TA and less disturbing to the students than formal in-class visitations by faculty; in addition, peer observations tend to be accurate, usually correlating well with SIR measures (Pica, Barnes, and Finger 1990). Also, TA peers may notice elements that undergraduate students miss in SIR evaluations and may be able to communicate their evaluations in a more forthright manner (Allen and Rueter 1990). Peer pairing of ITAs who have observed one another's classes also has proved to be an effective, non-threatening means of informal external assessment (N. Diamond and Visek 1991).

Self-evaluation. The use of self-evaluation of pedagogical and language skills has been more widely recommended in recent years. Various authors strongly promote a structured self-evaluation procedure for TAs and ITAs as an adjunct to various types of external evaluation (Allen and Rueter 1990; Pica, Barnes, and Finger 1990).

Especially recommended are self-evaluations made by the TA observations of audiotaped or videotaped classes—often in conjunction with a TA training program (Allen and Rueter 1990; Boehrer 1987; Brinton and Gaskill 1979; Franck and DeSousa 1982; Landa 1988; P. Lee 1987; Mestenhauser et al. 1980; Sarkisian 1984). Also strongly recommended are midterm self-evaluative measures that might serve as early warning signs to the TA that changes in his or her teaching behavior are indicated (Allen and Rueter 1990; Wulff, Staton-Spicer, Hess, and Nyquist 1985).

ITA Assessment
Compared with native English-speaking TAs, ITAs traditionally are considered less qualified in the areas of English language ability, teaching techniques appropriate for use with American undergraduate students, and the culture of the American university classroom. It is the ITA's English ability that usually has been the focus of undergraduate student criticism, as it may serve as the easiest target for the undergraduate who has had an unfavorable reaction to an ITA's cultural awkwardness as evidenced by his or her "foreign" teaching style and "strange" manner of interpersonal interaction (K. Bailey 1984; Dodd, Elbaum, Di Paolo, Adams, Hartmann, Huber, Kick, and Steiner 1989; Nelson 1990; Pialorsi 1984; Schneider and Stevens 1991; R. Smith et al. 1991; vom Saal 1987). Therefore, assessment of ITAs usually centers first on English language skills, with teaching skills and cultural knowledge of the American academic setting second.

It generally is agreed that before ITA candidates are provided the opportunity to take an ITA evaluative test of any type, they first should be able to demonstrate an adequate level of general English proficiency (K. Bailey 1984; Barrett 1987b; Byrd 1987b). Of the tests used to assess the ITA's general language ability, the TOEFL (Test of English as a Foreign Language) by far is the most widely used (Plakans and Abraham 1990); the MTELP (Michigan Test of English Language Proficiency) is the next most widely used.

In a survey of 96 universities, Johncock found that 96 percent of these use TOEFL for admission purposes, and the majority of these required a composite score of at least 550 (1987a). Administered 12 times a year in the U.S. and Canada and up to 12 times a year overseas by the Educational Testing Service (ETS), the objectively scored TOEFL yields a convenient composite score as well as three subscores: (1) structure and appropriate English usage; (2) listening comprehension; and (3) reading comprehension and vocabulary (*Bulletin: Overseas Edition* 1992; *Bulletin: U.S. and Canada Edition* 1992). The TOEFL contains no test of the productive skills of writing or speaking, although the TWE (Test of Written English) is offered free of charge at five of the TOEFL administrations.

Although Clark and Swinton note that there exists a fairly strong correlation between TOEFL scores and speaking proficiency on a group basis, they say that making "highly reliable statements about the speaking proficiency level of individual test candidates . . . on the basis of group correlational data (TOEFL scores) may be considered a rather questionable procedure" (1979, p. 1).

To be sure, the literature shows that TOEFL scores alone generally are considered inadequate by many for assessing the ITA's spoken English skills (Abraham and Plakans 1988; B. Davis 1987; Eck 1987). However, Dunn and Constantinides found that the TOEFL part score for the listening section was fairly reliable at predicting the ability of ITAs to perform adequate work in an ITA training course, but it was not a very good indicator of lack of success in the course. The TOEFL composite score, on the other hand, was fairly reliable in predicting lack of success in the training course, but it did not reliably predict success (Dunn and Constantinides 1991).

Tests used for the assessment of ITA language ability
The TSE. In October 1979, ETS brought out the Test of Spoken English (TSE) (Clark and Swinton, 1980). The TSE is

administered to groups by means of a prerecorded form of the test. It requires the examinee to provide various types of responses, such as reading aloud, completing sentences, describing a picture series, answering questions about a complex picture, responding to questions, and making announcements, to recorded cues (Stansfield and Ballard 1984). For those in need of a spoken English assessment, this test is administered around the world on the same dates as the TOEFL (*Bulletin: Overseas Edition* 1992; *Bulletin: U.S. and Canada Edition* 1992). Johncock's survey of 96 institutions showed that the TSE or its institutional version, the SPEAK (Speaking Proficiency English Assessment Kit), was required by only three universities for admission purposes (1987a).

Because the TSE is subjectively scored, the cost is high ($80) compared to the TOEFL ($35-42 in the U.S./Canada and $35-48 overseas). The TSE cost probably has discouraged many prospective ITAs from applying to institutions that require the TSE for admission (Barnes 1990; Plakans and Abraham 1990). The telephone interview has been suggested as a low-cost alternative to the TSE for departments that desire an informal evaluation of a prospective ITA's English-speaking ability (Barnes 1990; Fox, Berns, and Sudano 1989); others warn that its use has had limited success (Schneider and Stevens 1987).

The SPEAK test. The on-site test most widely used by U.S. colleges and universities is the SPEAK, a commercially available product of ETS consisting of retired forms of the TSE. Johncock's data showed that of the 60 institutions that used at least one type of test for ITA evaluation, 35 percent used the TSE and 40 percent used the SPEAK, whereas only 23 percent used the TOEFL (1987a). The $350 SPEAK consists of one retired form of the TSE along with 30 test booklets, 30 examinee handbooks, a cassette test tape, scoring key, 100 rating sheets, and elaborate rating and training tapes and materials for learning to score the SPEAK (*SPEAK* 1992; Stansfield and Ballard 1984). Three additional forms of the SPEAK that include 30 handbooks, 30 test books, and testing materials are available for $150 each (*SPEAK* 1992).

The initial acceptance of the SPEAK for on-site ITA testing is well-documented in the literature (Costantino 1988; Mellor 1987). Its popularity stems from its easy availability, widespread use that permits the comparison of results among user institutions, excellent rater training materials, and professionally prepared testing materials. Best of all, it is an easily administered, non-interactive test that can be provided to large groups of ITA candidates simultaneously in a language laboratory setting (Barrett 1987a; Plakans and Abraham 1990).

As with all subjectively rated tests, the quality and amount of training given to SPEAK raters is crucial to the success of such oral proficiency testing (Henning 1990; Mellor 1987). The test takes about 20 minutes to administer to a group and about 18 minutes per individual test to score.

The literature also shows a growing dissatisfaction with the SPEAK for various reasons. One often-cited reason is that the test does not adequately screen examinees, especially in the middle range of oral proficiency (Landa 1988). However, it is in this range that most ITA candidates fall (Plakans and Abraham 1990). Others have criticized the validity of the SPEAK as a means of testing oral communication on the grounds that human communication is clearly interactive, requiring at least two individuals who play the part of speaker and listener. The validity of the SPEAK also has been questioned in that it inadvertently tests listening comprehension in addition to oral production (Barrett 1987a; Brett 1987; Simon 1991). Due to these important considerations, many programs now use the SPEAK as a preliminary screening test followed by a second testing instrument that is interactive in nature and more sensitive in discriminating the middle range of spoken proficiency (Abraham, Klein, and Plakans 1986; Dalle and Inglis 1989; Gallego, Goodwin, and Turner 1991; Sequeira and Costantino 1989).

Detractors of the SPEAK also question its security due to the limited number of forms available (Barrett 1987a; Madsen 1990); its lack of relevance to classroom teaching or to the candidate's field (Carrell, Sarwark, and Plakans 1987; Schneider and Stevens 1987; Simon 1991); its reliance on sometimes balky or inferior audio equipment (Plakans and Abraham 1990); its time-consuming rating procedure, averaging about 18 minutes per rating (Plakans and Abraham 1990; Simon 1991); and irregularities and inconsistencies in the training materials and non-parallel forms of the test (Barrett 1987a). In addition, SPEAK does not provide for assessment of non-verbal communication skills, a major factor in confused communication across cultures.

Johnson describes Pennsylvania State University's attempt

to improve the SPEAK by dropping the first three sections, administering it face-to-face rather than in a language laboratory, making the response-time limits flexible, and by performing the rating during the administration (1991). The results so far have been very satisfactory. J. Smith reports on a study that compared the results of the SPEAK and a special field-specific SPEAK-like oral proficiency test (1989). No significant difference was found among ITAs' performance across the two tests, but some difference was noted in the pass/fail recommendations based on these results (J. Smith 1989).

Oral interviews. The oral interview is essentially a question-and-answer session conducted by one or more interviewers with a single examinee. It is this type of interactive, subjectively scored assessment instrument that often is chosen to supplement the use of the SPEAK (Plakans and Abraham 1990). One of the leaders among oral interviews is the ILR/ACTFL Oral Proficiency Interview, used by at least five institutions (Johncock 1987a). Originating with the U.S. government's Interagency Language Roundtable (ILR), a version of the ILR interview has been adopted by the American Council on the Teaching of Foreign Languages (ACTFL) for use in academic settings.

The interview, when administered by a highly trained interviewer, is capable of distinguishing 10 levels of oral language proficiency. The tape-recorded interview consists of four phases: warm-up, level check, probing for levels, and wind-down. For an advanced speaker, the ILR/ACTFL test might require 20 to 30 minutes to complete. Ratings of the interview are completed afterward from tape recordings and are based on factors such as pronunciation, vocabulary, grammar, and fluency (Plakans and Abraham 1990).

Although the ILR/ACTFL Oral Proficiency Interview is highly regarded as the most valid and reliable of currently used oral interviews, it is expensive, time-consuming, and difficult to administer and score (Mellor 1987). Most of the expense involves the extensive training and examiner certification required of the interviewers. Interviewer training is available only in week-long seminars offered five or six times a year. Since most ITA candidates generally would be considered advanced-level, the Oral Proficiency Interview would require up to a half hour per interview. Add to this the time needed to score the tapes of each interview (usually performed twice to enhance reliability), and it is clear that institutions with a large number of ITAs to evaluate would find the Oral Proficiency Interview impractical (Mellor 1987; Plakans and Abraham 1990).

More than half (58 percent) of the universities of the 60 surveyed by Johncock used an oral interview of some type—either alone or in conjunction with other evaluative instruments (1987a). (Note that oral communicative performance tests were included in this number.) Among those institutions that employ or have employed an oral interview for ITA assessment are the following: Southern Illinois University (Carrell, Sarwark, and Plakans 1987); the University of Wyoming, Emory University, the University of Pittsburgh, the University of Nevada-Reno, and the University of South Dakota.

Teaching simulation tests. The teaching simulation is another popular assessment tool for ITA evaluation (Barnes 1990; Byrd 1987b; Eck 1987; Paul 1991; Plakans 1989; R. Smith 1987). Johncock reported that 47 percent of the 60 institutions represented in his survey used a teaching simulation, including micro-teaching (1987a). In most cases, the ITA candidates are given a brief assignment related to their own fields to prepare a day in advance of their teaching performances.

When the ITA's teaching presentation—usually five to 10 minutes in length—occurs, it may be videotaped for later rating, presented to a live "class" made up of various people who ask questions and otherwise interact with the TA, or both (Plakans and Abraham 1990). The use of ESL professionals, undergraduate students, representatives from the ITA's department, and staff from the ITA training program as the TA's "class" adds some realism to the teaching situation and allows the participants to emphasize their own specific expertise and outlook in the rating process (Brett 1987; Briggs 1986; Johncock 1987b).

The teaching simulation may be scored for the ITA's use of English, ability to communicate ideas in English, presentation skills, interpersonal skills, and facilitation skills (Plakans 1989). If the rating is performed by ESL professionals alone, the scoring generally is limited to English language skills (pronunciation, grammar, and vocabulary), fluency, and facility of communication. Byrd cautions that because the videotaped teaching simulation is expensive and time-consuming, it should not be used as an initial screening device but only as a test of those ITA candidates who have demonstrated advanced oral English skills on other tests (1987b).

The teaching simulation has excellent face validity in that it appears to require the ITA candidate to do for assessment purposes just what he or she will be required to do in the classroom (Brett 1987; Byrd 1987b). However, the procedure can be inconvenient as well as expensive, especially if a diverse group of raters must be convened at a specific time and place to serve as pseudo "students" and raters (Byrd 1987b; Plakans 1989). It also should be noted that the reliability of the teaching simulation test depends directly on the quality of the training given to the raters who score the test (Plakans 1987).

Some institutions that use or have used the teaching simulation for ITA assessment—either alone or in conjunction with other tests—are Iowa State University (Abraham, Klein, and Plakans 1986); the University of Michigan (Briggs 1986); the University of Toledo (Eck 1987); Georgia State University (Byrd 1987b); Ohio State University (Carrell, Sarwark, and Plakans 1987); the University of Maryland (Aldridge, Palmer, and Lanier 1988); Wayne State University (Tipton 1990); the University of Minnesota (J. Smith, Dunham, K. Smith, Tzenis, Carrier, and Hendel 1991); the University of Wyoming, the University of Kentucky, the University of Nevada-Reno (Brett 1987); the University of Oklahoma (Paul 1991); Texas Tech University (R. Smith 1987); and Vanderbilt University, Mississippi State University, and the University of Iowa (Lyons 1989).

Oral communicative performance tests. Alternatives to the SPEAK, oral interview, and teaching simulation are found in a variety of oral communicative performance tests that require the ITA candidate to perform certain tasks that are thought to underlie the teaching skills needed in the classroom. Often the content of these tasks is related closely to the ITA's own field of study. Included among these tasks are the following: explaining a term or concept; summarizing, discussing, or explaining a field-specific article; reading aloud; pronouncing field-specific terms; describing or explaining a graph, diagram, picture, or chart; role-playing, including the management of office hours, simulated telephone conversations, and the performance of such classroom tasks as making an announcement, handling student questions, or giving

The reliability of the teaching simulation test depends directly on the quality of the training given to the raters who score the test.

assignments; and discussing pedagogical questions dealing with classroom management and student conduct. Oral communicative performance tests usually are administered by a single examiner and tape-recorded or videotaped for later scoring (Barrett 1989; Turner and Goodwin 1988).

Some of the main attractions of the oral communicative performance test are that it is interactive, flexible, and field-specific, unlike the SPEAK, and convenient to schedule, unlike the teaching simulation. More opportunity is provided to the candidate to show his or her versatility with a greater number of tasks than is provided by the oral interview alone. Like the oral interview, the oral communicative performance test has the advantages of easing the candidate's test anxiety, can be administered at a fairly low cost to the institution, and shows ease of administration (Plakans and Abraham 1990). As for disadvantages, tests with field-specific test materials (articles for discussion, technical terms for pronunciation, read-aloud paragraphs, and charts) require significantly more time and effort to prepare than materials for a general clientele.

Among institutions that use or have used oral communicative performance tests, either solely or in conjunction with other test instruments, are Michigan State University (Barrett 1986; Barrett 1987a); Emory University (Patricia Byrd, personal communication, June 23, 1992); and the University of California at Los Angeles (Gallego, Goodwin, and Turner 1991; Hinofotis, K. Bailey, and Stern 1981). Also included are the University of Texas-Austin (Simon 1991); the University of Michigan (Briggs 1986); the University of Pittsburgh (Cake and Menasche 1982); Drexel University; and the University of Pennsylvania (Hoekje and Linnell 1991).

Table 7 shows a summary of selected features of the TOEFL, the TSE, SPEAK, the teaching simulation, the oral interview, and the communicative performance test.

ITA Assessment Models and How They Are Used
The pre-training, pre-teaching screening test
The literature appears to support the premise that the large majority of the assessments dealing with ITA candidates can be categorized as pre-training, pre-teaching screening tests (Johncock 1987a). The candidates in this case already would have met institutional English-language requirements and would be qualified for full-time graduate study.

TABLE 7
SOME FEATURES OF ORAL PROFICIENCY TESTS

Features	TOEFL	TSE/SPEAK	Teaching Simulation	Oral Interview	Communicative Performance Test
Degree of relevance to specific ITA tasks	None	Low	High	Low	High
Degree of communicative interaction	None	None	Possibly high	High	Possibly high
Type of administration	Group	Group	Individual	Individual	Individual
Degree of expertise needed by examiners	Low	Low	Moderate	High	High
Degree of expertise required of raters	N/A	High	High	High	High
Availability of rater training materials	N/A	Yes	Possible	Possible	Possible
Test administration time	Fixed	Fixed	Flexible	Flexible	Flexible
Cost of equipment for administration/rating	Low	High	Possibly high	Low	Low
Degree of examinee's test anxiety	High	Very high	High	Low/Moderate	Moderate
Standardized test scores	Yes	Yes	No	No	No

In most cases, a screening test such as the SPEAK or an oral interview is used to measure oral English proficiency, largely due to the fact that most screening tests are administered and scored by ESL professionals. Less often, the screening tests also include measures of the candidate's teaching skills and cultural awareness of specific academic settings. Usually screening tests of this second type are in the form of simulated teaching or oral communicative performance tests that include raters not only from the ESL field but also from specific university departments and teaching specialties (Brett 1987; Briggs 1986; Johncock 1987a).

The use of the pre-training screening test often is three-fold: first, to determine whether a candidate is ready to begin teaching duties without prior training; second, if training is indicated, to diagnose the candidate's strengths and weaknesses and place the student in the appropriate level of an ESL or ITA training program; and third, to determine whether a candidate might qualify for an assistantship that requires less English proficiency, teaching skill, and crosscultural awareness than a classroom instructor, perhaps as a help-room tutor or a research assistant (Barrett 1989; R. Smith et al. 1991).

Figure 1 shows the progress of ITA candidates through a model university testing program that offers a combination of pre-teaching and pre-training screening tests.

The post-training screening test

Another common function of ITA assessment is the post-training screening test. Administered after the ITA candidate has completed a training program, the test may measure the candidate's mastery of various ESL, pedagogical, and cultural awareness content (that is, an achievement test) or it may measure the candidate's proficiency in these areas in the same way that such proficiency was measured in the pre-training screening test (that is, a parallel proficiency test). In any case, as a result of post-training testing, a determination can be made regarding which candidates have made enough progress to begin teaching assistantships and which candidates must repeat the training program or abandon their hopes of becoming ITAs (Sequeira and Costantino 1989; R. Smith et al. 1991).

Figure 2 describes how ITA candidates undergo both pre-training screening and placement and post-training testing within a model institutional program using an oral communicative performance test.

FIGURE 1

PRE-TRAINING, PRE-TEACHING SCREENING/ PLACEMENT COMBINATION ITA TESTS

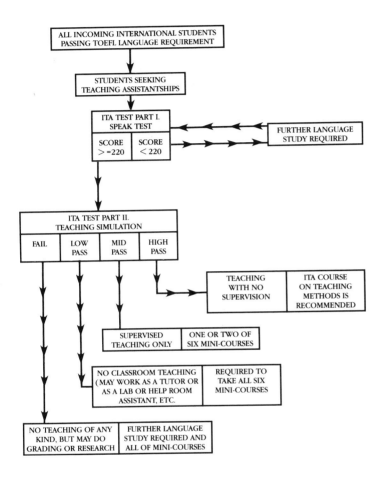

The concurrent-with-training screening test

The last type of ITA assessment—the screening evaluation
concurrent with training—is the most flexible. ITA candidates
are accepted into a training program and are administered
periodic tests of various types (SPEAK, simulated teaching,
and communicative performance tests, for example) during
the course of the program. At the end, the candidates' cumu-
lative test results and teachers' evaluations are used to determine whether the candidates will be recommended for teaching assistantships (R. Smith 1987; Yule and Hoffman 1990).

FIGURE 2

PRE-TRAINING SCREENING AND PLACEMENT AND POST-TRAINING ITA TESTS

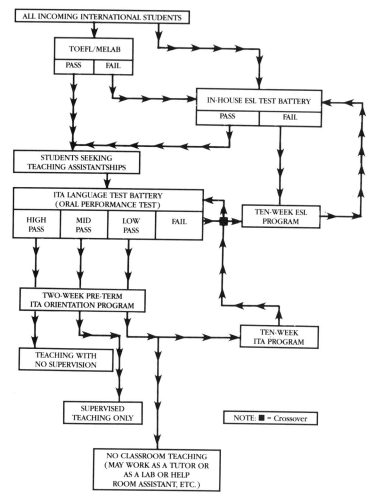

NOTE: MELAB = Michigan English Language Assessment Battery

Figure 3 details the flow of ITA candidates through a series of pre-training screening and concurrent-with-training tests in a model university testing-training program.

Evaluation of Training Programs

The National Survey of Teaching Assistant Training Programs and Practices was conducted in 1991 under the sponsorship

FIGURE 3

PRE-TRAINING SCREENING AND CONCURRENT-WITH-TRAINING ITA TESTING

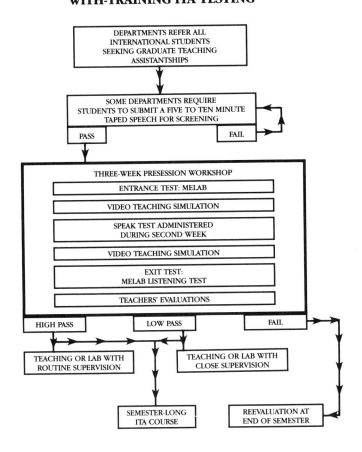

NOTE: MELAB = Michigan English Language Assessment Battery

of the American Association for Higher Education, Council of Graduate Schools, TIAA-CREF. Of the 206 institutions surveyed that had TA training programs in place, 52 percent have program evaluations of some kind (L. Lambert, Syverson, Hutchings, and Tice 1991).

End-of-term student instructional rating survey
The literature suggests that the most common type of evaluation technique for TA and ITA programs is the post-term

student instructional rating (SIR) survey completed by the students of TAs and ITAs (L. Lambert et al. 1991). Buerkel-Rothfuss and P.L. Gray (1990) noted that their survey of 164 graduate deans and 339 department heads indicated that 55.6 percent of the former and 42.1 percent of the latter used the end-of-term questionnaire for program evaluation. The assumption is that if the undergraduate students give their graduate assistant teachers good evaluations, the TA training program has succeeded in its purpose.

Questionnaires and survey forms are the usual means employed to gather information concerning overall teaching effectiveness of the TAs (Abraham and Plakans 1988; Bort and Buerkel-Rothfuss 1991b; Briggs and Hofer 1991; J. Kulik, C. Kulik, Cole, and Briggs 1985; and Mestenhauser et al. 1980). One-on-one interviews of a sampling of undergraduates also has been used, combined with other assessment instruments (Sequeira and Darling 1987).

Survey of TA/ITA participants and program staff

Another standard type of TA/ITA training program evaluation focuses on a survey of the teaching assistants' satisfaction with certain aspects of their program (Mestenhauser et al. 1980; Sequeira and Darling 1987; Stevens 1988; Turitz 1984). Buerkel-Rothfuss and P.L. Gray (1990) reported that of 164 graduate deans and 339 department heads surveyed, 66.7 percent of the deans and 19.4 percent of the department heads used an evaluation form completed by their teaching assistants (either alone or with the end-of-term questionnaire).

Areas commonly evaluated include the course content (ESL, pedagogical skills, and cultural knowledge); the activities (micro-teaching, demonstrations, role-playing, lecture presentations, lesson planning, and test writing and administration), the TA assessment measures used (tests, peer evaluation, and self-evaluation), and the staff (instructors and lecturers). This type of evaluation appears to be most commonly conducted with end-of-program questionnaires.

The same type of end-of-program evaluation involves a survey of the training program staff, sometimes including coordinators, session leaders, instructors, undergraduate student participants, and guest lecturers. A summary of the staff surveys and TA participant surveys provide valuable data for the improvement of future programs (Martin-Reynolds and Hurley 1987).

Survey of the TAs' departments

Another form of training program evaluation depends on the reports of department faculty who have made observational visits to TA classrooms. Buerkel-Rothfuss and P.L. Gray note that of the 164 graduate deans surveyed, 44.4 percent used faculty observations of TA/ITA teaching as an evaluation of their training programs, compared to only 36.1 percent of the 339 department heads (1990).

A less common form of program evaluation, carried out by the staff of centralized training programs, is a survey of the departments in which the TAs and ITAs teach. Department heads or course supervisors are interviewed regarding their opinions about the training program and how it might better serve their needs. Such close cooperation between training programs and the departments has resulted in a continuous revision and fine-tuning of the program's curriculum (Abraham and Plakans 1988; Schneider and Stevens 1987; Sequeira and Darling 1987).

Other Forms of Training Program Assessment

An alternative to surveys of the TAs or their students is the evaluation of the amount of progress (level of attainment) made by the students in the courses taught by the TAs. The degree to which the undergraduate students succeeded in their courses, as determined by their course grades, is taken as a measure of the success of their TAs' teaching effectiveness and indirectly of the TA training program (B. Davis 1987; Jacobs and Friedman 1988). Buerkel-Rothfuss and P.L. Gray reported that 5.6 percent of the 164 graduate deans and 14 percent of the 339 department heads surveyed used student academic performance as an evaluative indicator of the training program's quality (1990).

Bort and Buerkel-Rothfuss (1991b) offer an indirect form of program evaluation that involves a comparison of the evaluation items found on end-of-term SIR forms, checklists used by faculty when performing in-class observations, and end-of-term supervisors' evaluation forms, with the training categories identified in content analysis of TA training program materials (Bort and Buerkel-Rothfuss 1991a). Of 102 evaluation items found in an examination of 65 evaluation forms and 25 descriptions of evaluation procedures, only 54 percent were included in the TA training programs. Some dimensions of evaluation (such as facilitation skills, preparation, evaluation, and knowledge) were found to be well-covered in the training programs while other dimensions (such as professionalism, student feedback, and accessibility) were not. The authors conclude that careful decisions must be made regarding exactly which of the many possible evaluation items should be taught in TA training programs, which should be evaluated, and when and by what means evaluations should be obtained.

Summary

The assessment of TA/ITA teaching performance and the evaluation of training programs that support their teaching in U.S. undergraduate classes has shown impressive growth during the 1980s. However, a great deal remains to be accomplished with respect to the development of specific test types and formats for American TAs and ITAs. Further refinements are needed to increase the effectiveness of tests designed to assess needed English language skills, pedagogical skills, and cross-cultural sensitivity. Also, the coming decade undoubtedly will see the development of more efficient ways of evaluating the effectiveness of TA/ITA training programs. It is well to keep in mind that continuing research studies on TA and ITA teaching and training will be needed to inform these efforts, such as those typified in recent years by Myers and Plakans (1991); Rittenberg, Wieferich, Unkefer, and Leiserowitz (1988); and Williams, Barnes, Finger, and Ruffin (1987). However, the wide dissemination of such research results through future professional meetings and publications is no less important.

RESEARCH RELATED TO ITA TRAINING

Early in the development of ITA training programs, K. Bailey cautioned that the development of training had preceded a systematic investigation of issues related to international teaching assistants (1982). Since her call for additional research, the number of ITA studies gradually has increased, leading to the development of a small but important literature on various issues involved in the use of ITAs to teach undergraduate courses. In the following review, 32 of these studies are analyzed to reveal patterns and to suggest areas in which future research would be valuable.

Because the bulk of published work on ITAs involves reports on program design or testing issues rather than research, it was necessary to establish clear guidelines for selection of the work to be included in the following review of research: Any qualitative or quantitative study related to aspects of ITA training could be included. However, articles were excluded from this section of the text if they described existing programs, related to specific language proficiency testing issues, or pertained to foreign-language TAs who taught their first language (Spanish-speaking TAs who teach Spanish, for example).

Studies on program design issues are included in the third section of the text; testing is covered in the fourth section.

Research on ITAs in U.S. undergraduate education is a new field of study that crosses numerous disciplinary lines. In addition, ITA research is fragmented by the fact that there is no journal that is fully and consistently receptive to ITA papers. As a result, researchers must be more than usually persistent and inventive when seeking to carry out a thorough review of this relatively small literature.

The following four strategies are recommended as effective ways of identifying relevant research:

(1) The first strategy is the standard search through appropriate databases including MLA and Psychological Abstracts as well as ERIC. For this review, the ERIC search focused on articles published between 1966 and November 1991. The descriptors included such terms as "international," "foreign," and "non-native speaking teaching or research assistants," "FTA," "ITA," and "NNSTA." ERIC yielded 203 references, 83 of which related to non-ITA areas such as the international teaching alphabet, leaving at 120 the total number of references relating to international teaching assistants. Of that 120, by far the greatest number described ITA training programs

or dealt with TAs in foreign language departments. Only eight of the 120 references described ITA research related to ITA training.

(2) The second standard strategy is to check for doctoral dissertations in Dissertation Abstracts. A search through the period of 1966 to November 1991 yielded 23 references. Of these 23, two studies yielded no significant results, three were descriptive, three were not related to training, and four had been published, leaving 11 doctoral studies that focused on facets of ITA training.

(3) Because of the limited number of ITA research articles published in the standard professional journals, a productive third strategy is to consult published collections based on conferences and symposia. The current study analyzed the two publications that resulted from the national conferences on TA and ITA training—the first at Ohio State University (Chism and Warner 1987) and the second at the University of Washington (Nyquist et al. 1991); and the University of Michigan Bibliography (Briggs et al. 1990).

(4) Because of the relative newness of ITA research and, thus, a lack of recognized descriptors for use in computerized searches of bibliographic databases, it is realistically possible that important studies would not be identified easily by such a search. Therefore, the fourth strategy involves a manual search of national publications on international and higher education issues for articles that did not appear in ERIC.

These four strategies together yielded the 32 studies upon which the following discussion is based.

Upon analysis, five distinct categories emerged: studies related to (1) pronunciation, (2) effective teaching, (3) evaluation of ITA training programs, (4) the tasks ITAs perform, and (5) the concerns of ITAs themselves.

Studies Related to Pronunciation

ITA training developed, in part, in response to complaints about undergraduate students' inability to understand ITAs because of their pronunciation. As a result of these complaints, many early ITA training programs focused on pronunciation as the source of and solution to poor communication between ITAs and U.S. undergraduates. This emphasis on pronunciation has, in part, subsided. However, the issue of pronunciation continues to be troublesome, and trainers disagree about how much to emphasize it.

Six research studies focused on factors relating to undergraduates' perceptions of the ITAs' pronunciation. In an early study, Nisbitt and Wilson showed students a videotape of a Belgian presenting a lecture in one of two different styles (1977). In one videotape he was warm and friendly, while in the other he was cold and distant. Students rated the "warm" instructor's accent as attractive and the "cold" instructor's accent as irritating, thus suggesting that student evaluation of pronunciation is related to other variables besides pronunciation.

The role of other variables in students' perception of ITA pronunciation also is supported in a more recent study by Rubin (1992). Students listened to a four-minute audiotaped lecture by an American while viewing a slide of either an Oriental or a Caucasian. Students who viewed the Oriental slide perceived the lecturer's speech to be significantly more accented than those who viewed the Caucasian slide.

In a similar study, students heard either a highly or moderately accented audiotape of a Chinese speaker lecturing on science or the humanities and saw a photograph of either a Caucasian or an Oriental (Rubin and K. Smith 1990). Results suggest that students did not discriminate between the high or moderate accent and that factors such as instructor ethnicity and lecture topic were stronger determinants of student attitudes and comprehension than accented speech.

Brown also found that students' perception of ITAs' ethnicity affected the evaluation by students of language ability (1988, 1992). Undergraduates viewed a videotape of the same international speaker presenting a lecture but were offered different information about the ethnicity of the speaker. This information significantly affected their assessment of his pronunciation.

In a fifth study, Orth also investigated the influence of different factors on student evaluations of ITA language proficiency (1982). Results indicated that the subjects' evaluations of ITA language proficiency were related to their attitudes toward the course, their grade in the course, and the ITA's interest in them. Gallego examined undergraduate students' perceptions of communication breakdowns in ITA presentations (1990). Undergraduates identified pronunciation problems such as stress errors, the misuse of vocabulary, and speech flow as major factors contributing to communication breakdowns with ITAs.

Subjects' evaluations of ITA language proficiency were related to their attitudes toward the course, their grade in the course, and the ITA's interest in them.

In summary, these studies indicate that when students complain about an ITA's pronunciation, they also are responding to other variables. Some of these variables include the ITA'S warmth or coldness; the ethnicity of the ITA; the ITA's interest in the student; student attitude toward the course; and student satisfaction with grades.

Studies Related to Effective Teaching
Of the studies identified, 17 relate to effective ITA teaching behavior. Seven of the 17 studies used the qualitative methodology of discourse analysis; six of these seven used a measurement of teacher effectiveness such as student course evaluations. Three studies used discourse analysis without a teacher effectiveness measure, six used quantitative methodology and a teacher effectiveness measurement, and one used quantitative methodology without a teacher effectiveness measurement. Several of these studies contain pronunciation as a variable, but in addition, they examine other factors related to effective ITA teaching behavior.

Qualitative studies with a teacher effectiveness measurement
Seven of the identified studies investigated possible determinants for TA teaching success by analyzing classes taught by international and American TAs. All but one used a measure of teaching effectiveness (e.g., student evaluations, supervisors' recommendations) and then attempted to explicate the effective behavior by analyzing the spoken discourse of the TAs.

In an early study, K. Bailey used student evaluations of TAs' pronunciation, grammar, and vocabulary as a measure of teaching effectiveness (1982). By observing and taking qualitative field notes on 12 American and 12 international TAs, she found that American TAs who used more "bonding" (acts suggesting that the TA is trying to establish a bond) and "eliciting" moves (acts inviting student comments and questions) were rated more highly by students. Students did not prefer TAs who used "informing" moves (e.g., lecturing).

Gillespie also used student evaluations to measure teaching effectiveness (1988). She analyzed and coded the spoken discourse and non-verbal behavior of 11 American and international TAs and found no significant differences in the ways in which the two groups talked about classroom management issues, handled classroom discourse, answered questions, or used various communication strategies. Of the 11 TAs, the four highest rated TAs exhibited the greatest degree of eye contact with their students.

Rounds, using the TA supervisors' evaluations as a measure of teaching effectiveness, analyzed five 50-minute videotapes of American and international TAs (1987). Rounds found that successful TAs (1) more often use the word "we" and less often use the words "I" and "you," (2) elaborate more, (3) let students know when they are moving to a new subject, (4) use transitions between new and old information, (5) are clear about student responsibilities for the course, and (6) ask questions that begin an interaction.

Langham used two measures of TA effectiveness: (1) students' exam scores and (2) students' evaluations of the TAs (1989). She then analyzed the discourse of effective American and international TAs and concluded that effective teaching strategies include (1) establishing common ground, (2) providing a course overview, (3) defining terms and concepts, (4) reviewing the lesson, and (5) using the blackboard in an organized manner. Using student evaluations as measures of teaching effectiveness, Dege examined the discourse of successful and less successful ITAs (1983). Her findings suggest that successful ITAs use verbal behaviors that indicate agreement, support, and cooperation. They also smile and laugh more frequently.

Tyler, Jeffries, and Davies analyzed the spoken English discourse of 18 Korean and Chinese TAs who had been identified by undergraduates as difficult to understand (1988). They found that the Korean and Chinese TAs did not adhere to native speaker strategies of achieving coherence when presenting a lecture. Native speakers of American English orient listeners to the interrelationships among ideas by using (1) particular stresses, intonation patterns, and pauses, (2) subordinate clauses, and (3) words indicating the relationship between ideas such as *however, now, next,* and *anyway.* The Korean and Chinese speakers did not use these devices and were perceived by undergraduates as being disorganized and unfocused.

In a follow-up, in-depth analysis of one ITA/student interaction, Tyler and Davies found that a Korean ITA organized his response to a student's request for an explanation of a low grade in a manner that caused the student to misunderstand the ITA's message (1990). Tyler and Davies suggest that culture-specific preferences for certain organizational patterns of spoken discourse contribute to cross-cultural misunderstandings between ITAs and U.S. students.

The studies cited here suggest that American undergraduates prefer TAs who attempt to establish bonds or common ground, ask questions to begin interactions, look at students frequently, use the pronoun "we" often, let students know the organization of the class, indicate the relationships between ideas, are clear about student responsibilities, define terms and concepts, and use native English-speaker patterns of stress and intonation and native speaker organizational patterns of spoken discourse.

Qualitative studies without teacher effectiveness measurement

The next three studies are similar to the prior qualitative studies in that they compare American and international TAs and analyze spoken discourse in the classroom. They differ in that they do not attempt to measure teacher effectiveness. An apparent assumption behind these studies is that when teaching American students, the discourse of an effective ITA would resemble that of a native English-speaking TA.

Gillette analyzed and compared the communication strategies used by a Korean and an American TA giving an astronomy lecture (1982). The Korean used repetition to emphasize a concept and organized the lecture around a handout. The American used more gestures and eye contact and emphasized by restating a concept in different ways.

Tanner investigated the TA-student discourse of three American TAs and three international TAs, focusing on TA questions and student responses (1991a, 1991b). Results suggest the importance of questions in terms of student-TA interaction.

Katchen compared classroom behavior of American and Taiwanese TAs and their students, focusing on the verbal and non-verbal behavior of student-initiated question sequences (1990). Students asked the Taiwanese TAs fewer questions than they asked the American TAs. They also simplified the content and form of the questions for the Taiwanese TAs, suggesting an attempt to make themselves understood. The Taiwanese used more repetition in their answers than did the American TAs.

Quantitative studies with a teacher
effectiveness measurement

Six quantitative studies examined the relationship between ITA teaching effectiveness and specific teaching behaviors as measured by a quantitative instrument. Hinofotis and K. Bailey compared ESL instructor and student assessment of ITAs presented in a five-minute videotape during which they explained a term from their field to an interviewer (1981). The evaluation consisted of a Likert-scale and ranking instrument on Initial Overall Impression, Performance Categories, and Final Overall Impression and open-ended questions.

An analysis of student comments revealed that although they complained about language proficiency, they more frequently complained of the boring and monotonous qualities of the ITAs' explanations. In ranking 12 items from most to least important, both students and ESL faculty ranked pronunciation as the most important factor in the ITAs' intelligibility; however, they disagreed as to the importance of the category "Ability to Relate to Student." The students considered this item second in importance, while the ESL faculty placed it eighth. Both groups of raters had a strong preference for TAs who gave examples and illustrations.

Using a measure of communicator style, Inglis investigated the relationship between communicator style and student evaluations for 18 international TAs (1988). She found that only attentiveness—a willingness to provide feedback to students—correlated highly with student evaluations of ITAs. Other components of communicator style such as being dramatic, relaxed, and animated were not significant, suggesting that specific personality traits are less important to effective teaching than teacher-student interaction (e.g., being attentive to students and providing feedback).

In a third study using a quantitative measure of teaching effectiveness, W.E. Davis asked undergraduates to evaluate the teaching of international and native English speaking TAs by responding to statements regarding enthusiasm, rapport, approachability, and fairness by marking a five-point strongly agree/strongly disagree scale (1991). The statements represent teacher characteristics valued by American undergraduates and relate to teacher-student relationships. Students evaluated ITAs significantly lower than American TAs for all four characteristics, suggesting that undergraduates perceive ITAs to be less enthusiastic, approachable, and fair than American TAs.

Yule and Hoffman analyzed student evaluations, TOEFL scores, and GRE scores of ITAs in an attempt to predict which students would receive positive student evaluations (1990). Students with lower TOEFL and GRE verbal scores received more negative evaluations and those with higher TOEFL and GRE verbal scores received more positive recommendations.

The authors focused their discussion on TOEFL scores. They found that if only international graduate students with a TOEFL score of 570 or above had been granted teaching assistantships, more than half of those receiving negative evaluations would not have been teaching. If only those who received a TOEFL score of 625 had taught, all negative evaluations would have been avoided. However, at a score of 625, many students who received positive evaluations also would have been excluded.

The authors suggest that if academic departments have funding only for teaching assistants, then avoiding negative student evaluations is important and higher entry TOEFL scores are needed. However, if the department needs graduate TAs and has funding for non-teaching assistantships, lower TOEFL scores could be accepted. The authors conclude with a note that these ITAs had completed a 15-week training course, and that if they had not completed such a course, their evaluations would have been lower.

Two studies relating to teacher effectiveness concern the ITAs' culture. Keye found that when ITAs lectured on their culture rather than their field of study, students evaluated them significantly more positively (1981). Similarly, using videotapes of a male ITA lecturing, Nelson investigated the relationship between an ITA's use of cultural examples in lectures and student attitude and recall (1992). Using a free-recall technique to measure student learning and a teacher evaluation form, she found that students recalled significantly more of the lecture content and had a more positive attitude toward the ITA if he used cultural examples rather than hypothetical examples to illustrate concepts in his lecture.

These quantitative studies suggest that effective ITA teaching as measured by student evaluations or student learning (e.g., final exam scores) is related to language proficiency, teaching experience, and ITA training. These studies further point to the benefits of using specific teaching behaviors such as providing feedback to students, using examples and illustrations, and being open and approachable.

Quantitative studies without a teacher effectiveness measurement

One of the identified studies relates to the teaching effectiveness of ITAs but does not include a measurement of teaching effectiveness. Yule's study (1991) concerns the pedagogical issue of ITA/student difficulties in face-to-face interactions. He investigated the interactions of ITAs using an information-transfer task design in which one ITA (the sender) was instructed to describe a delivery route to another ITA (the receiver).

Each ITA was given a map showing city streets with buildings marked, but the maps were slightly different. ITAs could not see each others' maps. In this task, the sender is the information giver—a role similar to that of a teacher—and the receiver functions in a manner similar to a student, as a recipient of information. Analysis of the interactions indicated that if a sender had first been a receiver (i.e., listener), the sender was more likely to negotiate solutions than if the sender had not completed the task first as a receiver. Yule suggests that these results emphasize the importance of training ITAs in listening/speaking exercises where conflicts must be resolved and in listening itself.

Table 8 provides a list of the effective teaching behaviors that emerged from 14 of these studies. These behaviors can be roughly classified into three categories: those relating to (1) language proficiency, (2) interaction with students (e.g., asking students questions), and (3) the presentation of material (e.g., explaining the relationship between old and new information).

Studies Evaluating ITA Training Programs

Of the identified studies, four relate to ITA testing and training. These studies are connected closely to the effectiveness studies, in that the goal of testing and training is to assess and improve teacher effectiveness.

J. Kulik et al. compared student evaluations of newly appointed American and international TAs (1985). The ITAs received significantly lower ratings in four areas: overall excellence of instructor, clarity of instructor, rapport with the instructor, and overall excellence of course. However, an analysis of ITAs whose English was rated as proficient revealed that student ratings of these proficient ITAs were higher than

TABLE 8

FACTORS RELATING TO
EFFECTIVE TA AND/OR ITA TEACHING

Factor	Source
Having a certain level of English proficiency	Yule and Hoffman 1990
Establishing common ground between TA and students	Langham 1989
Providing feedback to students	Inglis 1988
Inviting student comments and questions	K. Bailey 1982
Asking students questions	Rounds 1987; Tanner 1991a, 1991b
Elaborating when explaining a concept	Gillette 1982; Langham 1989; Rounds 1987
Explaining the relationship between old and new information	Rounds 1987
Making student responsibilities clear	Langham 1989; Rounds 1987
Reviewing lessons	Langham 1989
Making eye contact with students	Gillespie 1988; Gillette 1982
Smiling and laughing	Dege 1983
Talking about their cultures	Keye 1981; Nelson 1992
Using appropriate stress, intonation, pauses, subordination, and transitions to achieve coherence in speaking	Tyler, Jeffries, and Davies 1988
Being friendly and interactive	K. Bailey 1982; Dege 1983; Hinofotis and K. Bailey 1981; Rounds 1987
Using the blackboard in an organized manner	Langham 1989

those of the non-proficient ITAs. In addition, students evaluated TAs and ITAs more highly their second term of teaching.

In a follow-up study, Briggs and Hofer (1991) examined whether student evaluations of ITAs changed as a result of mandatory university testing and training by comparing the post-training evaluations with the evaluations in the J. Kulik et al. (1985) study. Their results indicated that two items were significantly higher in the post-training study: (1) overall "my TA is an excellent teacher," and (2) "the instructor presents material clearly," suggesting that proficiency testing and follow-up training contribute to ITA effectiveness as perceived by undergraduate students.

In another study related to language testing and training, Jacobs and Friedman, using students taught by international and American TAs, examined the relationship between the ITAs' English proficiency scores and the achievement of and evaluations by students in five different courses (1988). Results indicated that TA nationality did not significantly affect final examination scores; in fact, students in three of the ITA-taught classes had higher mean scores on their final exams than students in sections taught by American TAs.

Results also revealed that in only one of the five courses did students evaluate the American TAs significantly higher than the ITAs. Finally, there was a significant correlation between an ITA's English proficiency score and students' performance on final exams and their ratings of instructors. The authors conclude that ITAs are as effective as American TAs, but they point out that the ITAs had been tested and screened for English proficiency.

In a longitudinal study, Stevens measured the effectiveness of an ITA training program that consisted of extensive video-taping, analyses of micro-teaching sessions, a drama-based approach, and wide use of undergraduate students (1988). Using five instruments to measure change in ITA skills including speaking, listening, and teaching abilities, Stevens found that the ITAs' oral proficiency and teaching skills had improved during training. In addition, the participants had acquired near native-like use of non-verbal behavior and had developed more positive teacher-student rapport.

The studies that assessed ITA testing and training point to the importance of both of these practices. Specifically, the results suggest the ITA testing and training are related to more positive student evaluations and to increased learning as measured by final exam scores. Effective training also improves ITA language proficiency and teaching skills. In addition, the results indicate that proficient ITAs are rated more highly than non-proficient ITAs, and ITAs are rated higher during their second term of teaching.

Studies Related to Tasks ITAs Perform

Two of the studies concern the tasks ITAs are expected to perform. In an examination of the tasks of lab assistants, Myers and Plakans observed 30 international lab assistants, interviewed the lab assistants and faculty, and transcribed tapes of actual discourse in labs (1991). Results revealed that the role of lab assistant is relatively undefined and that ITAs interact with students primarily by answering questions. ITAs varied greatly in the amount of TA-student interaction that occurred in the lab; some waited in the front of the lab for students to ask questions while others actively moved around the lab checking on student comprehension. Results also indicated diversity in required tasks according to the academic discipline and course level of the lab.

In another study related to the tasks ITAs are expected to perform, Williams et al. surveyed international and American TAs about the duties they were expected to perform, the skills needed for success, and problems they experienced (1987). Findings indicated that TA duties vary according to the department; TAs function as lab assistants and graders as well as teachers; ITAs are not frequently selected as teachers in their first year. These ITAs themselves reported that they had problems with pronunciation, stress, timing, and intonation.

These two studies suggest that ITA training is complicated by the varied tasks that ITAs perform. If most ITAs were lecturers, training could focus on lecturing; however, as these studies indicate, ITAs function as lab assistants and graders as well as teachers. ITA training programs need to train international graduate students for the varied positions they will be expected to fill.

Studies Related to the Concerns of ITAs

Three studies investigated the concerns and perceptions of ITAs. Bauer administered a quantitative instrument to 40 ITAs that focused on their concerns about (1) communication with undergraduates and (2) their roles as teachers (1991). The ITAs primarily were concerned with language-related issues such as pronunciation, vocabulary, clarity of expression, and understanding and responding to students' questions. They also expressed some worries about cultural issues such as using inappropriate humor in class and about their roles as teachers. For example, some raised concerns about lack of authority, lack of confidence, nervousness, and physical appearance.

Numrich investigated ITA values and attitudes concerning American undergraduates (1991). Her findings indicate that ITAs perceived that undergraduates were poorly prepared for academic work and not serious about their courses. She also found that ITAs were not pleased by the number of questions their students asked them in class.

In a third study examining ITA concerns, Ronkowski surveyed 88 international and 107 American TAs regarding attitudes about teaching styles, expectations of students, and views of teacher-student relationships (1987). This study also included follow-up interviews with 25 ITAs. Ronkowski found more similarities than differences in the points of view of American and international TAs; for example, both were surprised at how unprepared American undergraduates were for academic work. However, observers of two ITA-taught classes noted problems with classroom interaction patterns that the ITAs had not mentioned in the interviews, suggesting that the ITAs were either reluctant to discuss or unaware of potential problems in their classes.

A related implication is the need to prepare ITAs in American academic culture.

The results of the three studies in this category have implications for training. First, ITA concerns with language and cultural issues correspond to the content of most ITA training programs, suggesting that ITAs and ITA trainers have assessed the needs of ITAs in a similar manner.

A related implication is the need to prepare ITAs in American academic culture (e.g., undergraduates ask a lot of questions) and in American educational values such as providing the opportunity for a university-level education for as many students as possible. This practice of trying to educate the majority contrasts with the practice of educating the best and the brightest that exists in many other countries.

The third implication relates to the reliability of ITA self-report data, suggesting the importance of supervisors' observing ITA-taught classes.

Summary

In the late 1970s, when college students started writing letters to their university newspapers about not understanding ITAs, the students frequently cited pronunciation as the problem. The studies reviewed here suggest that undergraduates may have used the term "pronunciation" to cover a myriad of issues relating to the general foreignness of or their unfamiliarity with ITAs. That is not to say, however, that pronunciation is not an issue in ITA training. It appears that an ITA's pronunciation needs to be at a certain (undetermined) level of intelligibility for communication to occur, but beyond that level, other factors probably are more important.

This analysis of the research on ITAs provides a number of insights into factors other than pronunciation that are related to effective teaching. The results suggest the importance of interpersonal communication behaviors that relate to the relationship between the ITA and the student, behaviors such as being friendly and interactive, asking questions, and providing feedback to students. The educational literature also points to the importance of instructor-student relationships in American university classrooms.

Ard, reviewing research on the qualities of a good teacher, cites the importance of communication ability (1989). Good instructors are perceived to be enthusiastic, clear, open, relaxed, friendly, and sensitive to students' needs. Because the perceived qualities of good teachers vary from culture to culture, it is necessary to include American undergraduates' perceptions of good teachers in ITA training programs.

The 1970s have been referred to as the decade of faculty development and the 1980s as the decade of TA training. If the number of ITAs and ITA training programs continues to multiply, the 1990s may well be the decade of ITA training. Faculty development continued throughout the years that TA training gained momentum, and both will mature as ITA training moves forward. Unless unforeseen circumstances curb the current increase of international graduate students and international faculty at American universities, ITA training programs likely will multiply to meet the growing demands for effective international teaching assistants and faculty. Thus, the need continues for systematic investigation of issues related to ITAs and their U.S. undergraduate students.

CONCLUSION

Although the history of the graduate teaching assistantship in U.S. universities is not well-documented, Chase notes that graduate students were already being subsidized through undergraduate teaching assignments during the last decade of the 19th century (1970). He credits the shortage of qualified senior faculty in the period immediately after World War II as the single most important reason for the "TA System" becoming an established part of the U.S. research university. Within this system, basic undergraduate courses are taught by graduate students who are themselves usually enrolled in doctoral programs, but often in master's programs.

Changing demographics of scientific and technical education have led in the late 20th century to significant numbers of international students being selected as graduate teaching assistants and, thus, taking roles as teachers of U.S. undergraduates. With U.S. students turning to careers that do not require graduate study, U.S. research universities have found international students to be outstanding graduate students—often with better preparation in mathematics and other scientific and technical areas than their U.S. peers (*Everybody* 1989; R. Lambert 1993; Steen 1987).

For many U.S. students, parents, academics, and political leaders, this change is viewed as part of the crisis in undergraduate education stemming from an over-valuing of graduate education and the research function of the university and its faculty. These critics call for the use of regular full-time faculty in undergraduate courses rather than graduate teaching assistants. For other U.S. educators and political leaders, the increased presence of non-U.S. citizens implies a deflection of funding away from U.S. minority students. These critics would continue the use of graduate teaching assistants but would replace international students with U.S. minority students.

While the debate about the basic purposes and methods of the research university continues, institutions have continued to appoint international graduate students to teaching positions in undergraduate courses. This is due to the institution's interest in international educational exchange, to some small extent, but it primarily is due to the continuing shortage of qualified U.S. students.

To reply to the various criticisms about the English pronunciation and the teaching ability of ITAs, many institutions have found it wise, if not required, to establish assessment and training programs to improve the communication skills of ITAs. The resulting system of assessment and training for ITAs has grown rapidly, creating a strong record of experience and a small but growing body of research. These research studies provide a relatively consistent pattern of factors related to ITA pronunciation and effective teaching behaviors, showing that pronunciation is only one of many factors influencing communication between ITAs and U.S. undergraduates.

Certainly these studies and their findings are important first steps toward the development of research-based assessment and training programs for ITAs and for foreign faculty and for appropriate and effective orientation of U.S. undergraduates to increase their skills at communication with teachers and with other students from backgrounds different from their own.

Topics Needing Further Discussion and Research

Other areas are in need of investigation so that assessment and training can be based on accurate descriptions of the communication and teaching skills needed by ITAs and that programs of assessment and training can employ the most effective materials and methods. These areas include at least the following: (1) the characteristics of the undergraduate classroom, (2) methods and materials that make for successful ITA training and assessment, (3) the personal and professional results of training for international graduate students themselves, (4) the features of effective intercultural orientation for U.S. undergraduates, (5) assessment and training for international faculty members, and (6) policy planning issues.

Characteristics of the undergraduate classroom

Better understanding must be developed of the undergraduate classroom as an instructional setting. Those responsible for ITA training must finally come to terms with the identification of the specific linguistic, pedagogical, and cross-cultural skills that teachers of U.S. undergraduates need to be successful (Byrd and Constantinides 1992; Hoekje and Williams 1992).

What teaching tasks and skills are common to most disciplines, and which are specific to individual disciplines? It has been suggested that a baseline of accuracy and fluency in spoken English is necessary for effective teaching (K. Bailey 1982; Hoekje and Williams 1992). What is that base? How little English can a teacher know and still be an effective teacher?

How effective as teachers are ITAs as a group compared to U.S. TAs as a group?

Case study research could explore the complexity of the contexts in which ITAs and their U.S. students teach and learn. For example, it would be helpful to study both American undergraduates and ITAs in an ITA-taught class—beginning with their initial impressions and continuing until the end of the course. This research also could examine the effects on students of internationalization and multiculturalism in the classroom.

When these specifications are clearly established, methods of assessment and evaluation instruments can be developed or adapted specifically to meet individual program and institutional needs. These new tests then must be integrated into the various ITA training program models for maximum assessment power and efficiency.

ITA training and assessment

Few studies have been carried out to measure the effectiveness of specific ITA training programs or to examine the success of specific components of training programs such as videotaping or observing expert teachers. Nor has much evaluation been done of the testing systems and instruments that are used to evaluate the linguistic, pedagogical, and cultural knowledge of ITAs or potential ITAs.

A variety of assessment issues must be addressed in terms of development of appropriate test instruments and in evaluation of the results of these test systems. One aspect of this development should be a closer matching of the content of training programs and the specific evaluation items upon which assessment measures are based (Bort and Buerkel-Rothfuss 1991b). Another area in need of increased attention is the type of assessment test (TSE/SPEAK, oral interview, teaching simulation, or oral communicative performance test) that best fits a specific training program design (R. Smith et al. 1991). Research also is needed on ways to evaluate the effectiveness of the general and discipline-specific materials and teaching methods used in training programs.

Possible conflicts caused for the ITA by the training

The effect of training and possible "Americanization" on the ITAs themselves needs serious consideration (Rao 1989). Because teaching is deeply rooted in the culture of a society

(Hofstede 1986), it would be naive to believe that ITAs can adapt to teaching in an American classroom without conflict.

Study is needed to understand the processes the ITAs go through during training and their subsequent teaching experience. Questions that might be asked include: What kinds and how much resistance is there to training? Who adjusts easily? Who adjusts with difficulty? Is the cultural adjustment literature being used in training? If so, to what extent and with what effects?

Intercultural orientation for U.S. undergraduates

Assessment and training for ITAs have focused primarily on changes in the behaviors and attitudes of international graduate students. Study of U.S. undergraduates has attempted to clarify the nature of their problems in understanding the spoken English of their ITAs, suggesting that the roots of the problem lie in cultural and pedagogical differences that influence the capacities of the students to understand and to learn from teachers who are very different from themselves.

Study is needed of effective methods for orienting American students to different cultures, to cultural differences in classroom dynamics, and to strategies for more effective learning from an ITA (e.g., sitting near the front of the room, taking a more active role in learning by asking for clarification and repetition).

Although a few such training programs have been reported on (e.g, vom Saal 1987; R. Smith, Constantinides, and Hudson 1989), few research-based data are available on questions such as the following: What is the appropriate content for such training programs? How much time is needed to effect a change? What are reasonable goals or outcomes? What kinds of students are influenced by such programs? Are the programs effective? How might U. S. undergraduates change over time as a result of exposure to ITAs and/or exposure to intercultural orientation?

Assessment and training for international faculty

While the states of Texas and Iowa mandate assessment for all non-native speakers of English who have instructional roles, including faculty along with teaching assistants, few institutions in other states have yet acknowledged the potential for communication problems between their international faculty and their U.S. undergraduates. Questions remain regarding the political and legal ramifications of training and assessment for international faculty as well as the nature of the assessment and training that should be made available to international faculty.

Open Doors tracks the numbers of international students in U.S. colleges and universities; however, no such data are kept for faculty members. How many non-native speakers of English are now teaching in U.S. colleges and universities? What do they teach? Are their relationships with undergraduates any different from those relationships developed between ITAs and their undergraduate students?

Policy planning issues

Research also is needed on the ways in which institutions develop policies regarding ITA training and assessment, as well as the substance of those policies. Byrd, R. Smith, and Constantinides found, for example, that funding for ITA programs frequently is approached on an ad hoc basis, with many questions remaining concerning the adequacy and stability of funding for those programs (1990). Other policy issues include, for example, how institutions define and identify ITAs. What is the role or impact of ITA training and assessment on institutional goals for internationalization and multiculturalism? What kind of strategic planning is needed regarding the future role of ITAs in undergraduate instruction?

Required Administrative Support for Effective ITA Assessment and Training Programs

Effective ITA training programs depend, in large measure, on the quality and quantity of administrative support they receive. Administrators can support ITA training programs by (1) developing clearly defined, fair policies for assessment and training of ITAs and for implementation and enforcement of these policies; (2) providing stable and adequate funding for the programs; and (3) supporting scholarship focused on the various issues raised by ITA assessment and training.

In addition, administrators need to recognize and respect the needs and rights of the ITAs as well as the undergraduate students they teach. Top administrators also need to articulate—both within and outside of the university community—a balanced view of ITAs that acknowledges legitimate concerns without overlooking the important contributions that these international scholars make to our universities through their research and teaching (see, e.g., K. Bailey 1984; Pialorsi 1984).

The Future of ITA Assessment and Training

Institutions, professional associations, program administrators, and even individual faculty members are working to recruit more American students for U.S. graduate programs. Efforts are being made to improve the quality of mathematics instruction in U.S. public schools as well (Celis 1993). However, the current importance of international graduate students and international faculty to U.S. research universities is likely to continue long into the 21st century.

In addition, U.S. colleges and universities are rapidly changing to reflect the diversification of U.S. society so that undergraduates are likely to experience, in addition to their international instructors, increasing numbers of instructors who are not native speakers of English but who are U.S. residents and U.S. citizens. Indeed, the undergraduate student body itself is diversifying, so the "traditional" undergraduate student needs to be prepared to study with peers who are from many different linguistic and cultural backgrounds.

In the 21st century, U.S. research universities will continue to struggle with issues that are inherent in institutional structure: graduate vs. undergraduate education, research vs. teaching, faculty vs. administration, and institution vs. the community. Fundamental to all of these discussions is the change in the linguistic and cultural background of many of the participants. In this changing context, all of those—administrators, faculty, staff, and students—with responsibilities for the quality of an institution's educational, social, and cultural programs will find that they cannot assume that communication will occur.

Diversification and internationalization seem to be more than slogans; they are the generally used terms for processes that already are having substantial effect on the daily lives of those who work and study at U.S. universities, especially those in urban settings. Intercultural communication tells us that cultures in contact are cultures in conflict unless ongoing efforts are made to teach all involved in the encounters to develop and use improved strategies for communicating with each other.

Thus, ITA assessment and training are but two aspects of a much larger training effort that must be made at U.S. universities. Helping an international student to be a more accurate speaker of American English solves only part of the problem if U.S. undergraduates are still prepared to accept only white speakers of standard English as their preferred models for university teachers. To overcome that limited vision, ITA assessment and training program personnel must accumulate techniques and insights through which ITAs and U.S. students can learn to communicate meaningfully across the cultural, linguistic, pedagogical, and psychological boundaries that may separate them. Perhaps as importantly, successful ITA programs coupled with effective U.S. student orientation can provide models for the diversification and internationalization of the rest of the university.

REFERENCES

The Educational Resources Information Center (ERIC) Clearinghouse on Higher Education abstracts and indexes the current literature on higher education for inclusion in ERIC's data base and announcement in ERIC's monthly bibliographic journal, *Resources in Education* (RIE). Most of these publications are available through the ERIC Document Reproduction Service (EDRS). For publications cited in this bibliography that are available from EDRS, ordering number and price code are included. Readers who wish to order a publication should write to the ERIC Document Reproduction Service, 7420 Fullerton Rd., Suite 110, Springfield, VA 22153-2852. (Phone orders with VISA or MasterCard are taken at 800-443-ERIC or 703-440-1400.) When ordering, please specify the document (ED) number. Documents are available as noted in microfiche (MF) and paper copy (PC). If you have the price code ready when you call EDRS, an exact price can be quoted. The last page of the latest issue of *Resources in Education* also has the current cost, listed by code.

Abraham, Roberta G., and Barbara S. Plakans. 1988. "Evaluating a Screening/Training Program for NNS Teaching Assistants." *TESOL Quarterly* 22: 505-8.

Abraham, Roberta G., Craig Klein, and Barbara S. Plakans. 1986. "Beyond SPEAK: Testing Nonnative Teaching Assistants Under Classroom Conditions." Demonstration presented at the TESOL Convention, March, Anaheim, Calif.

Acton, William, Judy Gilbert, and Rita Wong. 1987. "A Practical Approach to Teaching Intonation and Rhythm." Paper presented at the TESOL Convention, April, Miami, Fla.

Adelman, Clifford. 1990. *A College Course Map: Taxonomy and Transcript Data.* Washington, D.C.: U.S. Department of Education.

Aldridge, Charlotte Groff, Leslie A. Palmer, and Lois Kleinhenn Lanier. 1988. "The Evaluation and Training Program for FTAs at the University of Maryland." Paper presented at the Symposium on the Training of International Teaching Assistants, April, University of Pennsylvania, Philadelphia.

Allen, R.R., and Theodore Reuter. 1990. *Teaching Assistant Strategies: An Introduction to College Teaching.* Dubuque, Iowa: Kendall-Hunt Publishing Company.

Althen, Gary. 1988. *Manual for Foreign Teaching Assistants.* Iowa City: University of Iowa Press.

American Society for Engineering Education. 1987. *A National Action Agenda for Engineering Education.* Washington, D.C.

Anderson-Hsieh, Janet. 1990. "Teaching Suprasegmentals to International Teaching Assistants Using Field-Specific Materials." *English for Specific Purposes* 9: 195-214.

Andrews, John. 1987a. "Department-Based and Centralized TA Training Programs." In *Institutional Responsibilities and Responses in the Employment and Education of Teaching Assistants: Readings from a National Conference,* edited by Nancy Van Note Chism and Susan Warner. Columbus: Center for Teaching Excellence, The Ohio State University.

———. 1987b. "Multiple Perspectives on the TAship: Part 1. A Developer's Perspective on Teaching in Higher Education: From Hobby to Profession." In *Institutional Responsibilities and Responses in the Employment and Education of Teaching Assistants: Readings from a National Conference,* edited by Nancy Van Note Chism and Susan Warner. Columbus: Center for Teaching Excellence, The Ohio State University.

"Answers to the Most Commonly Asked Questions Concerning the UIUC Policy Regarding the Oral English Proficiency of Classroom Instructors." 1988. Office of the Vice-Chancellor for Academic Affairs, Graduate College, University of Illinois at Urbana-Champaign.

Ard, Josh. 1989. "Grounding an ITA Curriculum: Theoretical and Practical Concerns." *English for Specific Purposes* 8: 125-38.

Ard, Josh, and John Swales. April 1986. "English for International Teaching Assistants: What ESL Institutes Can Offer." *TESOL Newsletter* 4: 21-2.

Axelson, Elizabeth, and Carolyn Madden. 1990. "Video-based Materials for Communicative ITA Training." *Issues and Developments in English and Applied Linguistics (IDEAL)* 5: 1-11.

Bailey, Kathleen M. 1982. "Teaching in a Second Language: The Communicative Competence of Non-Native Speaking Teaching Assistants." Ph.D. dissertation, University of California.

———. 1984. "The 'Foreign TA Problem.'" In *Foreign Teaching Assistants in U.S. Universities,* edited by Kathleen M. Bailey, Frank Pialorsi, and Jean Zukowski-Faust. Washington, D.C.: NAFSA.

Bailey, Kathleen M., Frank Pialorsi, and Jean Zukowski-Faust, eds. 1984. *Foreign Teaching Assistants in U.S. Universities.* Washington, D.C.: NAFSA. ED 249 843. MF-01.

Bailey, Stephen K., ed. 1977. *Higher Education in the World Community.* Washington, D.C.: American Council on Education.

Barnes, Gregory A. 1990. "A Bill of Rights for International Teaching Assistants." Paper presented at the TESOL Convention, March, San Francisco. ED 323 792. MF-01; PC-01.

Barnes, Gregory A., and Margaret van Naerssen. 1991. "Suggested Safety Issues/Communication Concerns for International Teaching Assistant Training." Paper presented at the NAFSA Conference, May, Boston.

Barrett, Ralph Pat. 1986. "Oral Interview for International Graduate Assistants." In *Working Papers,* edited by Janet C. Constantinides. Laramie, Wyo.: Wyoming/NAFSA Institute on Foreign TA Training.

———. June 1987a. "The SPEAK Test: Some Comments by a Former User." *NAFSA Newsletter:* 20-1.

———. 1987b. "The Testing and Evaluation of Foreign Teaching

Assistants: Where Are We and Where Are We Going?" In *Working Papers: Volume II*, edited by Janet C. Constantinides. Laramie, Wyo.: Wyoming/NAFSA Institute on Foreign TA Training.

———. 1989. "A Tool for Evaluating Language Proficiency of Foreign TAs." Paper presented at the TESOL Convention, March, Chicago, Ill.

Bauer, Gabriele. 1991. "Instructional Communication Concerns of International (Non-Native English-Speaking) Teaching Assistants— A Qualitative Analysis." In *Preparing the Professoriate of Tomorrow to Teach: Selected Readings in TA Training*, edited by Jody D. Nyquist, Robert D. Abbott, Donald H. Wulff, and Jo Sprague. Dubuque, Iowa: Kendall-Hunt Publishing Company.

Bernhardt, Elizabeth. 1987. "Training Foreign Teaching Assistants: Cultural Differences." *College Teaching* 35(2): 67-9.

Bland, Carole, and Constance C. Schmitz. 1988. "Faculty Vitality on Review: Retrospect and Prospect." *Journal of Higher Education* 59: 190-224.

Boehrer, J. 1987. "Suggestions for Watching Tapes with TAs." In *Institutional Responsibilities and Responses in the Employment and Education of Teaching Assistants: Readings from a National Conference*, edited by Nancy Van Note Chism and Susan Warner. Columbus: Center for Teaching Excellence, The Ohio State University.

Bolivar, Jeanette, and Susanne Sarwark. 1990. "Extending the Tutorial: Teacher-Made Individualized Practice Tapes." Demonstration presented at the TESOL Convention, March, San Francisco.

Bort, Mary B., and Nancy L. Buerkel-Rothfuss. 1991a. "A Content Analysis of TA Training Materials." In *Preparing the Professoriate of Tomorrow to Teach: Selected Readings in TA Training*, edited by Jody D. Nyquist, Robert D. Abbott, Donald H. Wulff, and Jo Sprague. Dubuque, Iowa: Kendall-Hunt Publishing Company.

———. 1991b. "Evaluating the Evaluation Forms: What Do We Expect from TA Teaching and How Are We Measuring What We Get?" Paper presented at the Third National Conference on the Training and Employment of Graduate Teaching Assistants, November, University of Texas, Austin.

Boyd, Frances. 1989. "Developing Presentation Skills: A Perspective Derived from Professional Education." *English for Specific Purposes* 8(2): 195-203.

Boyd, Frances, Linda Lane, and Polly Merdinger. 1989. *Resources for International Teaching Assistant Programs Teaching and Administrative Materials*. Columbia University: American Language Program.

Boyer, Ernest. 1991. *Scholarship Reconsidered: Priorities of the Professoriate*. Princeton, N.J.: The Carnegie Foundation for the Advancement of Higher Education.

Brett, Sally. 1987. "Screening Tests for Training Programs for Foreign

Teaching Assistants: An Examination of Rationale." In *Working Papers: Volume II*, edited by Janet C. Constantinides. Laramie, Wyo.: Wyoming/NAFSA Institute on Foreign TA Training.

Briggs, Sarah L. 1986. "Report on FTA Evaluations, 1985-86." Internal report. Ann Arbor: ELI Testing Division, The University of Michigan.

Briggs, Sarah L., and Barbara Hofer. 1991. "Undergraduate Perceptions of ITA Effectiveness." In *Preparing the Professoriate of Tomorrow to Teach: Selected Readings in TA Training*, edited by Jody D. Nyquist, Robert D. Abbott, Donald H. Wulff, and Jo Sprague. Dubuque, Iowa: Kendall-Hunt Publishing Company.

Briggs, Sarah L., Sunny Hyon, Patricia Aldridge, and John Swales. 1990. *The International Teaching Assistant: An Annotated Critical Bibliography*. Ann Arbor: English Language Institute Publications, The University of Michigan. ED 323 852. MF-01 PC-04.

Brinton, Donna, and William Gaskill. 1979. "A Language Skills Orientation Program for Foreign Teaching Assistants and Graduate Students." *Workpapers in Teaching English As a Second Language* 13: 49-68. ED 199 994. MF-01; PC-01.

Brown, Kimberley. 1988. "Effects of Perceived Country of Origin, Educational Status, and Native Speakerness on American College Student Attitudes Toward Non-Native Instructors." Ph.D. dissertation, University of Minnesota.

———. 1992. "American College Student Attitudes Toward Nonnative Instructors." *Multilingua* 11: 249-65.

Brown, Kimberley, Phillip F. Fishman, and Nancy L. Jones. 1990. "Foreign Teaching Assistant Speech Tests: Are You Breaking the Law?" *International Educator* 1: 8-12.

———. 1991. "Language Proficiency Legislation and the ITA." In *Preparing the Professoriate of Tomorrow to Teach: Selected Readings in TA Training*, edited by Jody D. Nyquist, Robert D. Abbott, Donald H. Wulff, and Jo Sprague. Dubuque, Iowa: Kendall-Hunt Publishing Company.

Bryson, John M. 1988. *Strategic Planning for Public and Nonprofit Organizations: A Guide to Strengthening and Sustaining Organizational Achievement*. San Francisco: Jossey-Bass.

Buerkel-Rothfuss, Nancy L., and Pamela L. Gray. 1990. "Graduate Teaching Assistant Training in Speech Communication and Noncommunication Departments: A National Survey." *Communication Education* 39: 292-307.

———. 1991. "Teaching Assistant Training: The View from the Top." In *Preparing the Professoriate of Tomorrow to Teach: Selected Readings in TA Training*, edited by Jody D. Nyquist, Robert D. Abbott, Donald H. Wulff, and Jo Sprague. Dubuque, Iowa: Kendall-Hunt Publishing Company.

Bulletin of Information for TOEFL/TWE and TSE 1992-93: Overseas Edition. 1992. Princeton, N.J.: Educational Testing Service.

Bulletin of Information for TOEFL/TWE and TSE 1992-93: United

States and Canada Edition. 1992. Princeton, N.J.: Educational Testing Service.

Burn, Barbara, ed. 1980. *Expanding the International Dimension of Higher Education.* San Francisco: Jossey-Bass.

Byrd, Patricia. 1987a. "Academic Sub-Cultures within U.S. Higher Education: Implications for FTA Training of Differences in Teaching Styles and Methods." In *Working Papers,* edited by Janet C. Constantinides. Laramie, Wyo.: Wyoming/NAFSA Institute on Foreign TA Training.

———. 1987b. "Being Seduced by Face Validity: Linguistic and Administrative Issues in Videotaped Teaching Simulation Testing." In *Institutional Responsibilities and Responses in the Employment and Education of Teaching Assistants: Readings from a National Conference,* edited by Nancy Van Note Chism and Susan Warner. Columbus: Center for Teaching Excellence, The Ohio State University.

Byrd, Patricia, and Janet C. Constantinides. 1988. "FTA Training Programs: Searching for Appropriate Teaching Styles." *English for Specific Purposes* 7: 123-29.

———. 1992. "The Language of Teaching Mathematics: Implications for Training ITAs." *TESOL Quarterly* 26(1): 163-7.

Byrd, Patricia, Phyllis Hurt, and Janet C. Constantinides. 1988. "Saying It Right: Key Vocabulary and FTA Lecturing." Paper presented at the TESOL Convention, March, Chicago.

Byrd, Patricia, Janet C. Constantinides, and Martha Pennington. 1989. *The Foreign Teaching Assistant's Manual.* New York: Collier MacMillan.

Byrd, Patricia, Rosslyn M. Smith, and Janet C. Constantinides. 1990. "Patchwork Quilts of Funny Money: Funding for Foreign Teaching Assistant Programs in the U.S." *Journal of Intensive English Studies* 4: 1-19.

Cage, M. 1991. "States Questioning How Much Time Professors Spend Working with Undergraduate Students." *Chronicle of Higher Education* 37(47): 1, A20.

Cake, Cathy, and Lionel Menasche. 1982. "Improving the Communication Skills of Foreign Teaching Assistants." Paper presented at the NAFSA Conference, May, Seattle. ED 225 373. MF-01; PC-01.

Carrell, Patricia, Susanne Sarwark, and Barbara Plakans. 1987. "Innovative ITA Screening Techniques." In *Institutional Responsibilities and Responses in the Employment and Education of Teaching Assistants: Readings From a National Conference,* edited by Nancy Van Note Chism and Susan Warner. Columbus: Center for Teaching Excellence, The Ohio State University.

Celis, William. 3rd ed. January 1, 1993. "U.S. Trails Japan and Taiwan in Math." *New York Times.* A11.

Chandler, Alice. 1989. *Obligation or Opportunity: Foreign Student*

Policy in Six Major Receiving Countries. New York: Institute of International Education.

Chase, John L. 1970. *Graduate Teaching Assistants in American Universities: A Review of Recent Trends and Recommendations.* U.S. Office of Education, Washington, D.C.: U.S. Government Printing Office.

Chism, Nancy Van Note, and Susan Warner, eds. 1987. *Institutional Responsibilities and Responses in the Employment and Education of Teaching Assistants: Readings from a National Conference.* Columbus: Center for Teaching Excellence, The Ohio State University. ED 292 783. MF-01.

Civikly, Jean M., and Dennis M. Muchisky. 1991. "A Collaborative Approach to ITA Training: The ITAs, Faculty, TAs, Undergraduate Interns, and Undergraduate Students." In *Preparing the Professoriate of Tomorrow to Teach: Selected Readings in TA Training,* edited by Jody D. Nyquist, Robert D. Abbott, Donald H. Wulff, and Jo Sprague. Dubuque, Iowa: Kendall-Hunt Publishing Company.

Clark, John L.D., and Spencer S. Swinton. 1979. *An Exploration of Speaking Proficiency Measures in the TOEFL Context.* TOEFL Research Report No. 4, Princeton, N.J.: Educational Testing Service.

———. 1980. *The Test of Spoken English As a Measure of Communicative Ability in English-Medium Instructional Settings.* TOEFL Research Report No. 7, Princeton, N.J.: Educational Testing Service. ED 218 960. MF-01; PC-04.

Cohen, Robby, and Ron Robin, eds. 1985. *Teaching at Berkeley: A Guide for Foreign Teaching Assistants.* Graduate Assembly of the University of California, Berkeley. ED 289 384. MF-01.

Constantinides, Janet C. 1985. "Improving the Comprehensibility of Foreign TAs." Paper presented at the NAFSA Conference, May, Baltimore.

———, ed. 1986. *Working Papers.* Laramie, Wyo.: Wyoming/NAFSA Institute on Foreign TA Training.

———. 1987a. "Designing a Training Program for International Teaching Assistants." In *Institutional Responsibilities and Responses in the Employment and Education of Teaching Assistants: Readings From a National Conference,* edited by Nancy Van Note Chism and Susan Warner. Columbus: Center for Teaching Excellence, The Ohio State University.

———. 1987b. "Providing Classroom English Communication Skills for Foreign Graduate Assistants." Paper presented at meeting of the Midwestern Association of Graduate Schools, March, Chicago.

———. 1987c. "Where Should We Go From Here: Research Needs Relating to Training Programs for FTAs." Paper presented at the NAFSA Conference, May, Long Beach, Calif.

———, ed. 1987d. *Working Papers: Volume II.* Laramie, Wyo.: Wyoming/NAFSA Institute on Foreign TA Training.

———. 1988a. "Typology of Training Programs for Non-Native Speak-

ers of English (NNSE)." Paper presented at meeting of the Western
Association of Graduate Schools, March, Reno, Nev.

―――. 1988b. "A Typology of International TA Training Programs."
Paper presented at SIETAR (Society for Intercultural Education,
Training, and Research), May, Denver.

Constantinides, Janet C., and Patricia Byrd. 1986. "Foreign TA's: What's
the Big Problem?" *Journal of International Student Personnel*
3: 27-32.

Coombs, Phillip. 1985. *The World Crisis in Education: The View From
the Eighties.* New York: Oxford University Press.

Costantino, Magdalena. March 1986. "Foreign TA Training: Penn
State's Cross-Cultural Communication Module." *NAFSA Newsletter.*
12-13.

―――. 1988. "Performance of International Students on the SPEAK
Test: Research Report." Paper presented at the Symposium on the
Training of International Teaching Assistants, April, University of
Pennsylvania, Philadelphia.

Creswell, J. October 11, 1990. "Oral Communication Competence
Causes Debate at UI." *The Daily Iowan:* 1A.

Dalle, Theresa S., and Margaret J. Inglis. 1989. "What Really Affects
Undergraduates' Evaluations of Nonnative Teaching Assistants'
Teaching?" Paper presented at the TESOL Convention, March, San
Antonio, Texas. ED 310 641. MF-01; PC-01.

Davey, Kathleen B., and Curt Marion. 1987. "Evaluating TA Development Programs: Problems, Issues, Strategies." In *Institutional
Responsibilities and Responses in the Employment and Education
of Teaching Assistants: Readings from a National Conference,*
edited by Nancy Van Note Chism and Susan Warner. Columbus:
Center for Teaching Excellence, The Ohio State University.

Davies, Catherine, and Andrea Tyler. 1989. "Demystifying Cross-
Cultural Miscommunication: Positive Results from 'Negative Evi-
dence.'" Paper presented at the TESOL Convention, March, San
Antonio, Texas.

Davis, Brian. 1987. "The Effectiveness of Videotaped Protocols as
a Training Technique for International TAs." In *Institutional Responsibilities and Responses in the Employment and Education of
Teaching Assistants: Readings from a National Conference,* edited
by Nancy Van Note Chism and Susan Warner. Columbus: Center
for Teaching Excellence, The Ohio State University.

Davis, William E. 1991. "International Teaching Assistants and Cultural
Differences: Student Evaluations of Rapport, Approachability,
Enthusiasm and Fairness." In *Preparing the Professoriate of Tomor-
row to Teach: Selected Readings in TA Training,* edited by Jody
D. Nyquist, Robert D. Abbott, Donald H. Wulff, and Jo Sprague.
Dubuque, Iowa: Kendall-Hunt Publishing Company.

Dege, Dolores Bolon. 1983. "Verbal and Nonverbal Communication
Behaviors in Multicultural Groups: An Exploratory Analysis." Ph.D.

dissertation, University of Minnesota.

DePalma, Anthony. April 21, 1992. "As Black Ph.D.'s Taper Off, Aid for Foreigners is Assailed." *New York Times*: 1, A9.

Diamond, Nancy, and Priscilla Visek. 1991. "Beyond the First Semester: Self-Evaluation for Experienced TAs." Paper presented at the Third National Conference on the Training and Employment of Graduate Teaching Assistants, November, University of Texas, Austin.

Diamond, Robert M., and Peter J. Gray. 1987. "A National Study of Teaching Assistants." In *Institutional Responsibilities and Responses in the Employment and Education of Teaching Assistants: Readings from a National Conference*, edited by Nancy Van Note Chism and Susan Warner. Columbus: Center for Teaching Excellence, The Ohio State University. ED 292 360. MF-01.

Dodd, David H., Batya Elbaum, Marianna Di Paolo, A. Adams, Barbara Hartmann, D. Huber, E. Kick, and R. Steiner. 1989. "Are International Graduate Students Less Effective as College Teaching Assistants Than American TAs?" Paper presented at the Second National Conference on the Training and Employment of Teaching Assistants, November, University of Washington, Seattle.

Dodge, Susan. October 23, 1991. "Surge of Students from Asia and Eastern Europe Lifts Foreign Enrollments in U.S. to Record 407,500." *Chronicle of Higher Education*, 38(9): A39-40.

Douglas, Dan, ed. 1990. *English Language Testing in U.S. Colleges and Universities*. Washington, D.C.: NAFSA.

Douglas, Dan, and Cynthia Myers. 1987. *Teaching Assistant Communication Strategies*. Videotape. Ames: Iowa State University. Includes manual, 18 pp.

Duba-Biedermann, Lisa. 1991. "Changes in Teaching Behavior Reported by Teaching Assistants After a Midterm Analysis of Teaching." In *Preparing the Professoriate of Tomorrow to Teach: Selected Readings in TA Training*, edited by Jody D. Nyquist, Robert D. Abbott, Donald H. Wulff, and Jo Sprague. Dubuque, Iowa: Kendall-Hunt Publishing Company.

Dunkel, Patricia A., and Tannaz Rahman. 1987. "Developing Listening and Speech Communication Skills: A Course for Prospective International Teaching Assistants." In *Institutional Responsibilities and Responses in the Employment and Education of Teaching Assistants: Readings from a National Conference*, edited by Nancy Van Note Chism and Susan Warner. Columbus: Center for Teaching Excellence, The Ohio State University.

Dunn, Thomas G., and Janet C. Constantinides. 1991. "Standardized Test Scores and Placement of International Teaching Assistants." In *Preparing the Professoriate of Tomorrow to Teach: Selected Readings in TA Training*, edited by Jody D. Nyquist, Robert D. Abbott, Donald H. Wulff, and Jo Sprague. Dubuque, Iowa: Kendall-Hunt Publishing Company.

Eble, Kenneth. 1983. *The Aims of College Teaching*. San Francisco: Jossey-Bass.

Eck, John S. 1987. "Screening International TAs for Oral English Proficiency." In *Institutional Responsibilities and Responses in the Employment and Education of Teaching Assistants: Readings From a National Conference*, edited by Nancy Van Note Chism and Susan Warner. Columbus: Center for Teaching Excellence, The Ohio State University.

"Efforts Needed to Fill Language Gap." October 12, 1988. *Arizona Daily Wildcat*: 4.

Elder, Kevin A. May 15, 1977. "A Modest Proposal." *Minnesota Daily*: np.

English Language Institute. 1991. ELI Brochure. Ann Arbor: The University of Michigan.

Erickson, Glenn R. 1986. "A Survey of Faculty Development Practices." In *To Improve the Academy*, edited by Marilla D. Svinicki, Joanne Kurfiss, and J. Stone, vol. 5. A joint publication of the Professional and Organizational Development Network in Higher Education and the National Council for Staff, Program, and Organizational Development. Stillwater, Okla.: New Forums Press, Inc.

Everybody Counts: A Report to the Nation on the Future of Mathematics Education. 1989. Washington, D.C.: National Academy Press.

Fiske, E.B. June 4, 1985. "When Teachers Can't Speak Clear English." *New York Times*: C1, C6.

Florida English Language Proficiency Act of 1983. SB 7-B, sec. 19.

Ford, James E., Lavon Gappa, Judy Wendorff, and Delivee L. Wright. 1991. "Model of an ITA Institute." In *Preparing the Professoriate of Tomorrow to Teach: Selected Readings in TA Training*, edited by Jody D. Nyquist, Robert D. Abbott, Donald H. Wulff, and Jo Sprague. Dubuque, Iowa: Kendall-Hunt Publishing Company.

Fox, Wanda. 1991. "Functions and Effects of International Teaching Assistants at a Major Research Institution." Ph.D. dissertation, Purdue University.

Fox, Wanda, Margie Berns, and Gary Sudano. 1989. "Assessing the Communicative Competence of ITAs: The Telephone Interview." Paper presented at the Second National Conference on the Training and Employment of Teaching Assistants, November, University of Washington, Seattle.

Franck, Marion R., and Michael A. DeSousa. 1982. "Foreign TAs: A Course in Communication Skills." *Improving College and University Teaching* 30(3): 111-4.

"Full-Time Employees by Race." August 28, 1991. *Almanac*: 29. Washington, D.C.: *Chronicle of Higher Education*.

Gaff, Jerry G., and David O. Justice. 1978. "Faculty Development Yesterday, Today, and Tomorrow." *Institutional Renewal Through the Improvement of Teaching*, edited by Jerry G. Gaff. New Directions for Higher Education No. 24. San Francisco: Jossey-Bass.

Gallego, Juan Carlos. 1990. "The Intelligibility of Three Nonnative English-Speaking Teaching Assistants: An Analysis of Student-Reported Communication Breakdowns." *Issues in Applied Linguistics* 1: 219-37.

Gallego, Juan Carlos, Janet Goodwin, and Jean Turner. 1991. "ITA Oral Assessment: The Examinee's Perspective." In *Preparing the Professoriate of Tomorrow to Teach: Selected Readings in TA Training,* edited by Jody D. Nyquist, Robert D. Abbott, Donald H. Wulff, and Jo Sprague. Dubuque, Iowa: Kendall-Hunt Publishing Company.

Gass, Susan, and Evangeline M. Varonis. 1984. "The Effect of Familiarity on the Comprehensibility of Nonnative Speech." *Language Learning* 34: 65-89.

Gburek, Janice L., and Stephen C. Dunnett, eds. 1986. *The Foreign TA: A Guide to Teaching Effectiveness.* State University of New York, Buffalo. ED 285 512. MF-01; PC-03.

Gillespie, Junetta K. 1988. "Foreign and U.S. Teaching Assistants: An Analysis of Verbal and Nonverbal Classroom Interaction." Ph.D. dissertation, University of Illinois.

Gillette, Susan. 1982. "Lecture Discourse of a Foreign TA: A Preliminary Needs Assessment." In *ESL Working Papers,* edited by Kathryn A. Winkler, No. 2. Minneapolis: University of Minnesota. ED 250 907. MF-01; PC-01.

Gottschalk, E.C. October 17, 1985. "Foreign Student-Teacher Faulted for Lack of Fluency in English." *Wall Street Journal:* 31.

Gottschalk, Katherine K. 1991. "Training TAs Across the Curriculum to Teach Writing: Embracing Diversity." In *Preparing the Professoriate of Tomorrow to Teach: Selected Readings in TA Training,* edited by Jody D. Nyquist, Robert D. Abbott, Donald H. Wulff, and Jo Sprague. Dubuque, Iowa: Kendall-Hunt Publishing Company.

Graham, Janet G. 1992. "Bias-free Teaching as a Topic in a Course for International Teaching Assistants." *TESOL Quarterly* 26(3): 585-9.

Greenfield, R. 1990. *Developing International Education Programs.* San Francisco: Jossey-Bass.

Gruber, Carol S. 1975. *Mars and Minerva: World War I and the Uses of the Higher Learning in America.* Baton Rouge: Louisiana State University Press.

Gunesekera, Manique, and John Swales. 1987. *The Office Hour: Materials for Foreign Teaching Assistants.* Ann Arbor: English Language Institute, University of Michigan. Accompanying videotape.

Hahn, Laura D. 1989. "An Intensive Orientation Program for International Teaching Assistants." Paper presented at the TESOL Convention, March, San Antonio, Texas.

Harari, Maurice. 1983. *Internationalizing the Curriculum and the Campus: Guidelines for the AASCU Institutions.* Washington, D.C.: American Association of State Colleges and Universities.

Heller, Scott. September 11, 1985. "Colleges Try Tests and Training to Make Sure Foreign TA's Can Be Understood." *Chronicle of Higher Education* 31(2): 1+.

———. 1986. "Teaching Assistants Get Increased Training; Problems Arise in Foreign-Student Programs." *Chronicle of Higher Education* 33(9): 12-13.

Henke, James. 1987. "Policies for Graduate Assistants in the English Graduate Program at Youngstown State University." In *Institutional Responsibilities and Responses in the Employment and Education of Teaching Assistants: Readings from a National Conference*, edited by Nancy Van Note Chism and Susan Warner. Columbus: Center for Teaching Excellence, The Ohio State University.

Henning, Grant. 1990. "Interpreting Test Scores." In *English Language Testing in U.S. Colleges and Universities*, edited by Dan Douglas. Washington, D.C.: NAFSA.

Hinofotis, Frances B., and Kathleen M. Bailey. 1981. "Undergraduates' Reactions to the Communication Skills of Foreign Teaching Assistants." In *On TESOL '80: Building Bridges: Research and Practice in Teaching English as a Second Language*, edited by Janet C. Fisher, Mark A. Clarke, and Jacquelyn Schacter. Washington, D.C.: TESOL. ED 208 643. MF-01.

Hinofotis, Frances B., Kathleen M. Bailey, and Susan L. Stern. 1981. "Assessing the Oral Proficiency of Prospective Foreign Teaching Assistants: Instrument Development." In *Selected Papers From the Colloquium for Oral Proficiency Testing at the 1979 TESOL Convention*, edited by Adrian S. Palmer, Peter J.M. Groot, and George H. Trosper. Washington, D.C.: TESOL. ED 223 111.

Hoekje, Barbara, and Kimberly Linnell. 1991. "Language Evaluation and Performance Testing for International Teaching Assistants." Paper presented at the Third National Conference on the Training and Employment of Graduate Teaching Assistants, November, University of Texas, Austin.

Hoekje, Barbara, and Jessica Williams. 1992. "Communicative Competence and the Dilemma of International Teaching Assistant Education." *TESOL Quarterly* 26(2): 243-69.

Hofstede, Geert. 1986. "Cultural Differences in Teaching and Learning." *International Journal of Intercultural Relations* 10: 301-20.

Hudson-Ross, Sally, and Yu Ren Dong. 1990. "Literacy Learning as a Reflection of Language and Culture: Chinese Elementary School Education." *The Reading Teacher* 44: 110-23.

Inglis, Margaret A. 1988. "Variables That Affect Undergraduates' Evaluations of Non-Native Speaking Teaching Assistants' Instruction." Ph.D. dissertation, Memphis State University.

Inglis, Margaret, and Teresa Dalle. 1992. "ITA 'Teacher Talk': Discourse Markers as Guideposts to Learning." Paper presented at TESOL conference, March, Vancouver, British Columbia, Canada.

Jacobs, Lucy C., and Charles B. Friedman. 1988. "Student Achievement

---

Under Foreign Teaching Associates Compared with Native Teaching Associates." *Journal of Higher Education* 59: 552-63.

Jenkins, Hugh M., ed. 1983. *Educating Students from Other Nations.* San Francisco: Jossey-Bass.

Jenkins, Susan, and Don Rubin. 1991. "International Teaching Assistants' Stereotypes of American Minority Group Students: The Next Crisis in Higher Education?" Paper presented at the 3rd National Conference on the Training and Employment of Graduate Teaching Assistants, November, University of Texas, Austin.

Johncock, Phil. 1987a. "FTA Tests and University Testing Policies." In *Working Papers: Volume II*, edited by Janet C. Constantinides. Laramie, Wyo.: Wyoming/NAFSA Institute on Foreign TA Training.

———. 1987b. "Graduate School Instructional Development International Teaching Assistant (ITA) Training Project." Draft of 1987-88 Annual Report, University of Nevada-Reno. Document obtained from the Wyoming Clearinghouse for FTA Training Materials, Department of English, University of Wyoming, Laramie.

Johnson, Karen. 1991. "Modifying the SPEAK Test for International Teaching Assistants." *TESOL Matters* 1(1): 8.

Johnson, Karen, Patricia Dunkel, and Deborah Rekart. 1991. "Use of Computer Technology in ITA Training Programs." Paper presented at the Third National Conference on the Training and Employment of Graduate Teaching Assistants, November, University of Texas, Austin.

Katchen, Johanna E. 1990. "The Other Side of Classroom Discourse: What Happens When the Students are Native Speakers and the Teacher Uses L2?" In *Issues in Applied Linguistics* 1: 219-37.

Kelley, J. June 18, 1982. "Foreign Teachers Bring Language Problems to U.S. Campuses." *Los Angeles Times.* Part I-C, 12.

Kerr, Clark. 1980. "Introduction: Global Education Concerns of Higher Education for the 1980s and Beyond." In *Expanding the International Education of Higher Education*, edited by Barbara Burn. San Francisco: Jossey-Bass.

Keye, Fatma Z.A. 1981. "An Exploratory Study of Students' Written Responses to International Teaching Assistant Presentations." Ph.D. dissertation, University of Minnesota.

Kuh, G.D., and E.J. Whitt. 1988. *The Invisible Tapestry: Culture in American Colleges and Universities.* ASHE-ERIC Higher Education Report No. 1, Washington, D.C.: Association for the Study of Higher Education.

Kulik, James A., Chen-Lin C. Kulik, Margaret A. Cole, and Sarah L. Briggs. 1985. "Student Evaluations of Foreign Teaching Assistants." Internal report, Center for Research on Learning and Teaching, University of Michigan, Ann Arbor.

Lambert, Leo M., Peter D. Syverson, Pat Hutchings, and Stacey Lane Tice. 1991. "1991 Survey of Teaching Assistant Programs: An Overview of Current Practices." Paper presented at the Third National

Conference on the Training and Employment of Graduate Teaching
Assistants, November, University of Texas, Austin.

Lambert, Leo, and Stacey L. Tice, eds. 1993. *Preparing Graduate Students to Teach: A Guide to Programs That Improve Undergraduate Education and Develop Tomorrow's Faculty.* Washington, D.C.: American Association for Higher Education.

Lambert, Richard D. 1993. "The Impact of Foreign Graduate Student Flows on American Higher Education." *NAFSA: Association of International Educators Newsletter* 44(3): 1, 7+. (The complete text of this article, which is an extraction of an address, is available as NAFSA Working Paper #37.)

Landa, Mark. 1988. "Training International Students as Teaching Assistants." In *Culture, Learning, and the Disciplines: Theory and Practice in Cross-Cultural Orientation,* edited by Josef A. Mestenhauser, Gayla Marty, and Inge Steglitz. Washington, D.C.: NAFSA.

Langham, Claire K. 1989. "Discourse Strategies and Classroom Learning: American and Foreign Teaching Assistants." Ph.D. dissertation, University of California.

Lawrence, Joyce V. 1987. "Fostering and Monitoring TA Development: What Administrators Can Do." In *Institutional Responsibilities and Responses in the Employment and Education of Teaching Assistants: Readings from a National Conference,* edited by Nancy Van Note Chism and Susan Warner. Columbus: Center for Teaching Excellence, The Ohio State University.

Lay, Nancy, and Linda H. Mantel. 1987. "ESL Workshop for Graduate Students at the City College of New York, CUNY." In *Institutional Responsibilities and Responses in the Employment and Education of Teaching Assistants: Readings from a National Conference,* edited by Nancy Van Note Chism and Susan Warner. Columbus: Center for Teaching Excellence, The Ohio State University.

Lay, Nancy, Linda H. Mantel, and Ellen Smiley. 1991. "International Teaching Assistants and International Students: Dimensions of the T.A. Experience in a Multicultural Institution." Paper presented at the Third National Conference on the Training and Employment of Graduate Teaching Assistants, November, University of Texas.

Lee, Motoko, Mokhar Abd-Ella, and Linda Burks. 1981. *Needs of Foreign Students from Developing Nations at U.S. Colleges and Universities.* Washington, D.C.: NAFSA.

Lee, Peter. 1987. "Video Use in FTA Training Programs: A Survey." In *Working Papers: Volume II,* edited by Janet C. Constantinides. Laramie, Wyo.: Wyoming/NAFSA Institute on Foreign TA Training.

"Let's Talk It Over: Foreign TAs, U.S. Students Fight Culture Shock." December 1985. *Newsweek on Campus:* 43-44.

Linnen, Beth. December 5, 1977. "Complaints about TA Teaching Prompt Probe." *Minnesota Daily:* np.

Lowman, Joseph. 1984. *Mastering the Techniques of Teaching.* San Francisco: Jossey-Bass.

Lyons, Michael. 1989. "Brief Overviews of the FTA Programs at Some Participants' Universities." Paper presented at Wyoming/NAFSA Institute on Foreign TA Training, July, University of Wyoming, Laramie.

Madden, Carolyn, and Cynthia Myers. Forthcoming. *Discourse and Performance of International Teaching Assistants.* Alexandria, Va.: TESOL.

Madsen, Harold S. 1990. "Standardized ESL Tests Used in U.S. Colleges and Universities." In *English Language Testing in U.S. Colleges and Universities*, edited by Dan Douglas. Washington, D.C.: NAFSA.

Mangan, Katherine S. January 15, 1992a. "Surge of Chinese to U.S. Colleges Defies Effort Aimed at Restricting Study Abroad." *Chronicle of Higher Education*: A38-39.

————. March 4, 1992b. "Colleges Expand Efforts to Help Teaching Assistants Learn to Teach." *Chronicle of Higher Education*: A17-18.

Mantel, Linda. 1989. "Overview of Problems and Suggested Solutions Related to the Assessment and Training of Teaching Assistants in Biology and Chemistry at City College." Proposal presented at the Wyoming/NAFSA Institute for Foreign TA Training, July, Laramie, Wyo.

Martin-Reynolds, Joanne, and Marian Smith Hurley. 1987. "The Graduate Student Orientation Program at Bowling Green State University." In *Institutional Responsibilities and Responses in the Employment and Education of Teaching Assistants: Readings from a National Conference*, edited by Nancy Van Note Chism and Susan Warner. Columbus: Center for Teaching Excellence, The Ohio State University.

McKeachie, Wilbert. 1978. *Teaching Tips: A Guidebook for the Beginning College Teacher.* Lexington, Mass.: D.C. Heath and Company.

McMillen, Liz. October 29, 1986. "Teaching Assistants Get Increased Training: Problems Arise in Foreign Student Programs." *Chronicle of Higher Education* 33(9): 9-11.

Mellor, Jeff. 1987. "Standard Oral Proficiency Tests for International Graduate Teaching Assistants." In *Institutional Responsibilities and Responses in the Employment and Education of Teaching Assistants: Readings from a National Conference*, edited by Nancy Van Note Chism and Susan Warner. Columbus: Center for Teaching Excellence, The Ohio State University.

————. 1988. *Some Steps to Improve Your Spoken English.* Knoxville: The University of Tennessee. ED 292 297. MF-01; PC-01.

Mestenhauser, Josef A., William Perry, Michael Paige, Mark Landa, Susanna Brutsch, Dolores Dege, Kenneth Doyle, Susan Gillette, Gail Hughes, Ronald Judy, Zehra Keye, Kathryn Murphy, Jan Smith, Kay Vandersluis, and Jon Wendt. 1980. "Report of a Special Course for Foreign Student Teaching Assistants to Improve Their Classroom Effectiveness." International Student Adviser's Office and

Program in ESL, University of Minnesota.

Molotsky, I. 1985. "Ohio May Test Foreign Graduate Students." *Footnote: A Publication of the American Association of University Professors*, Fall 4.

Monoson, Patricia, and Clayton Thomas. 1991. "Policy Directed at International Teaching Faculty in Institutions of Higher Education: An Analysis of Oral English Language Proficiency Policies." Paper presented at the Third National Conference on Graduate Teaching Assistants, November, University of Texas, Austin.

Mooney, Carolyn J. April 25, 1990. "Universities Awarded Record Number of Doctorates Last Year: Foreign Students Thought to Account for Much of the Increase." *Chronicle of Higher Education*, 36(32): 1+.

Morley, Joan. 1991. "Perspectives on English for Academic Purposes." In *Georgetown University Round Table on Languages and Linguistics 1991*: 1-22.

Morris, Frank L. 1991. "American Minorities and International Students: Striking What Balance?" An Address to the Plenary Session of the Council of Graduate Schools, December, Washington, D.C.

Myers, Cynthia, and Dan Douglas. 1991. "The ITA as Lab Assistant: Strategies for Success." Paper presented at the NAFSA Conference, May, Boston.

Myers, Cynthia, and Barbara Plakans. 1990. "The Discourse Community of the University Scientific Laboratory." Paper presented at the TESOL Convention, March, San Francisco.

———. 1991. " 'Under Controlled Conditions': The ITA As Laboratory Assistant." In *Preparing the Professoriate of Tomorrow to Teach: Selected Readings in TA Training*, edited by Jody D. Nyquist, Robert D. Abbott, Donald H. Wulff, and Jo Sprague. Dubuque, Iowa: Kendall-Hunt Publishing Company.

National Research Council. 1987. *Strengthening U.S. Engineering Through International Cooperation: Some Recommendations for Action*. Washington, D.C.: National Academy Press.

———. 1988. *Foreign and Foreign-Born Engineers in the United States: Infusing Talent, Raising Issues*. Washington, D.C.: National Academy Press.

Nelson, Gayle L. 1990. "International Teaching Assistants: A Review of Research." Paper presented at the TESOL Convention, March, San Francisco. ED 321 535. MF-01; PC-01.

———. 1992. "The Relationship Between the Use of Personal, Cultural Examples in International Teaching Assistants' Lectures and Uncertainty Reduction, Student Attitude, Student Recall, and Ethnocentrism." *International Journal of Intercultural Relations* 16: 33-52.

New York Times. May 12, 1992. A22.

Nisbett, Richard E., and Timothy D. Wilson. 1977. "The Halo Effect: Evidence for Unconscious Alteration of Judgments." *Journal of*

Personality and Social Psychology 35: 250-6.

Numrich, Carole A. 1991. "The Impact of Attitudes and Values on the Instructional Performance of International Teaching Assistants." Ph.D. dissertation, Columbia University Teachers College.

Nyquist, Jody, Robert D. Abbott, Donald H. Wulff, eds. 1989. *Teaching Assistant Training in the 1990s.* New Directions for Teaching and Learning No. 39. San Francisco: Jossey-Bass.

Nyquist, Jody D., Robert D. Abbott, Donald H. Wulff, and Jo Sprague, eds. 1991. *Preparing the Professoriate of Tomorrow to Teach: Selected Readings in TA Training.* Dubuque, Iowa: Kendall-Hunt Publishing Company.

Oklahoma English Proficiency Act of 1982. Titl. 70 OS Sup. Sec. 3224-5.

Olsen, Leslie, and Thomas Huckin. 1991. *Technical Writing and Professional Communication for Nonnative Speakers of English.* 2d. ed. New York: McGraw-Hill.

Open Doors: A Report on Three Surveys: Foreign Students, Foreign Faculty Members, Foreign Doctors. 1955. New York: Institute of International Education.

Open Doors 1984-85. 1985. New York: Institute of International Education.

Open Doors 1989-90. 1990. New York: Institute of International Education.

Open Doors 1990-91. 1991. New York: Institute of International Education.

Orth, John L. 1982. "University Undergraduates Evaluational Reactions to the Speech of International Teaching Assistants." Ph.D. dissertation, University of Texas.

Parsons, Adelaide H., and L. Szelagowski. March 1983. "Communication Skills for International Teaching Associates at Ohio University." *NAFSA Newsletter.* 114-6+.

Paul, Janis. 1991. "The TEACH Test: A Better Way of Ensuring ITA English Skills." Paper presented at the Third National Conference on the Training and Employment of Graduate Teaching Assistants, November, University of Texas, Austin.

Pialorsi, Frank. 1984. "Toward an Anthropology of the Classroom: An Essay on Foreign Teaching Assistants and U.S. Students." In *Foreign Teaching Assistants in U.S. Universities,* edited by Kathleen M. Bailey, Frank Pialorsi, and Jean Zukowski-Faust. Washington, D.C.: NAFSA.

Pica, Teresa, Gregory A. Barnes, and Alexis G. Finger. 1990. *Teaching Matters: Skills and Strategies for International Teaching Assistants.* Rowley, Mass.: Newbury House Publishers.

Pickert, Sarah M. 1991. *Preparing for a Global Community: Achieving an International Perspective in Higher Education.* ASHE-ERIC Higher Education Report No. 92-2, Washington, D.C.: Association for the Study of Higher Education.

Plakans, Barbara S. 1987. "A Plan for Training the Raters of a Teaching Simulation Test." In *Working Papers: Volume II*, edited by Janet C. Constantinides. Laramie, Wyo.: Wyoming/NAFSA Institute on Foreign TA Training.

————. 1989. "Teaching Simulations for ITA Testing." Paper presented at the Second National Conference on the Training and Employment of Teaching Assistants, November, University of Washington, Seattle.

Plakans, Barbara S., and Roberta G. Abraham. 1990. "The Testing and Evaluation of International Teaching Assistants." In *English Language Testing in U.S. Colleges and Universities*, edited by Dan Douglas. Washington, D.C.: NAFSA.

Pons, Cathy R. 1987. "A Three-Phase Approach to TA Training: The Program for Associate Instructors in French at Indiana University." In *Institutional Responsibilities and Responses in the Employment and Education of Teaching Assistants: Readings from a National Conference*, edited by Nancy Van Note Chism and Susan Warner. Columbus: Center for Teaching Excellence, The Ohio State University.

Puhl, C., Alexis G. Finger, and Gregory A. Barnes. 1983. "Training Foreign TAs: The Material(s) Possibilities." Paper presented at the TESOL Convention, March, Toronto, Ontario, Canada.

Rao, Shashi Kulkarni. 1989. "The Long Shadow of Neocolonialism: Experiences of Asian Students on the American Campus." Ph.D. dissertation, The Pennsylvania State University.

Rittenberg, William, Mary Ann Wieferich, Virginia Unkefer, and Antony Leiserowitz. 1988. "FTAs at Work: A Pilot Study on TA Training and Classroom Performance." Paper presented at the Symposium on the Training of International Teaching Assistants, April, University of Pennsylvania, Philadelphia.

Ronkowski, Shirley. 1987. "International and American TAs: Similarities and Differences." In *Institutional Responsibilities and Responses in the Employment and Education of Teaching Assistants: Readings from a National Conference*, edited by Nancy Van Note Chism and Susan Warner. Columbus: Center for Teaching Excellence, The Ohio State University.

Ronkowski, Shirley, with Margaret McMurtrey, Jiaying Zhuang, and Karen Myers. 1986. *An International Teaching Assistant Handbook: An Introduction to University and College Teaching in the United States*. Santa Barbara: Office of Instructional Consultation, University of California.

Rosen, Debra. September 29, 1977. "Ridiculous." *Minnesota Daily*: np.

Rounds, Patricia L. 1985. "Talking the Mathematics Through: Disciplinary Transaction and Socio-Educational Interaction." Ph.D. dissertation, University of Michigan.

————. 1987. "Characterizing Successful Classroom Discourse

for NNS Teaching Assistant Training." *TESOL Quarterly* 21: 643-71.

Rouvalis, Cristina. December 22, 1986. "Say That Again...: Foreign Lecturers are Hard to Understand, Students Complain." *Pittsburgh Post-Gazette.* 1+.

Rubin, Donald L. 1992. "Nonlanguage Factors Affecting Undergraduates' Judgments of Nonnative English Speaking Teaching Assistants." *Research in Higher Education* 33: 511-31.

Rubin, Donald L., and Kim A. Smith. 1990. "Effects of Accent, Ethnicity, and Lecture Topic on Undergraduates' Perceptions of Nonnative English-Speaking Teaching Assistants." *International Journal of Intercultural Relations* 14: 337-53.

Sadow, Stephen A., and Monica A. Maxwell. 1983. "The Foreign Teaching Assistant and the Culture of the American University Class." In *On TESOL '82: Pacific Perspectives on Language Learning and Teaching,* edited by Mark A. Clarke and Jean Handscombe. Washington, D.C.: TESOL. ED 228 897.

Sarkisian, Ellen. 1984. "Training Foreign Teaching Assistants: Using Videotape to Observe and Practice Communicating and Interacting With Students." In *On TESOL '84: A Brave New World for TESOL,* edited by Penny Larsen, Elliott L. Judd, and Dorothy S. Messerschmitt. Washington, D.C.: TESOL. ED 274 190. MF-01; PC-01.

Schneider, Katharine S., and Scott G. Stevens. 1987. "Curriculum Considerations for a Campus-Wide International Teaching Associate Training Program." In *Institutional Responsibilities and Responses in the Employment and Education of Teaching Assistants: Readings from a National Conference,* edited by Nancy Van Note Chism and Susan Warner. Columbus: Center for Teaching Excellence, The Ohio State University.

————. 1991. "American Undergraduate Students as Trainers in an International Teaching Assistant Training Program." In *Preparing the Professoriate of Tomorrow to Teach: Selected Readings in TA Training,* edited by Jody D. Nyquist, Robert D. Abbott, Donald H. Wulff, and Jo Sprague. Dubuque, Iowa: Kendall-Hunt Publishing Company.

Secter, Bob. September 27, 1987. "Foreign Teachers Create Language Gap in Colleges." *Los Angeles Times.* 1.

Sequeira, Debra L. 1990. "Effecting Instructional Change with Foreign Faculty: Consultation as a Research Process." Paper presented at the NAFSA Conference, May, Portland, Ore.

Sequeira, Debra L., and Magdalena Costantino. 1989. "Issues in ITA Training Programs." In *Teaching Assistant Training in the 1990s,* edited by Jody D. Nyquist, Robert D. Abbott, and Donald H. Wulff. New Directions for Teaching and Learning No. 39. San Francisco: Jossey-Bass.

Sequeira, Debra L., and Ann L. Darling. 1987. "A Multi-Perspective Approach to International Teaching Assistant Training: The International Teaching Assistant Project of the Center for Instructional Development and Research, University of Washington." In *Institutional Responsibilities and Responses in the Employment and Education of Teaching Assistants: Readings from a National Conference*, edited by Nancy Van Note Chism and Susan Warner. Columbus: Center for Teaching Excellence, The Ohio State University.

Shaw, E. February 15, 1982. "No Comprende! Foreign TAs Try to Cope with English." *The Daily Pennsylvanian*: 3.

Simon, Terry. 1991. "Evaluating the English Oral Proficiency of ITAs." Paper presented at the Third National Conference on the Training and Employment of Graduate Teaching Assistants, November, University of Texas, Austin.

Smith, Jan. 1989. "Topic and Variation in ITA Oral Proficiency: SPEAK and Field-Specific Oral Tests." *Journal of English for Specific Purposes* 8: 155-67.

———. 1992. "Enhancing Curricula for ITA Development." Paper presented at the TESOL Convention, March, Vancouver, British Columbia, Canada.

Smith, Jan, Trudy Dunham, K. Smith, Connie Tzenis, Carol Carrier, and Darwin Hendel. 1991. "Evaluation of the Teaching Effectiveness of International Teaching Assistants Who Participated in the Teaching Assistant English Program." Paper presented at the Third National Conference on the Training and Employment of Graduate Teaching Assistants, November, University of Texas, Austin.

Smith, Jan, Colleen Meyers, and Amy J. Burkhalter. 1992. *Communicate: Strategies for International Teaching Assistants*. Englewood Cliffs, N.J.: Prentice Hall Regents.

Smith, Rosslyn M. 1987. "Training International TAs at Texas Tech: An Overview." In *Institutional Responsibilities and Responses in the Employment and Education of Teaching Assistants: Readings from a National Conference*, edited by Nancy Van Note Chism and Susan Warner. Columbus: Center for Teaching Excellence, The Ohio State University.

———. 1989. "Culture in FTA Training Programs: An Overview." Paper presented at the Wyoming/NAFSA Institute for Foreign TA Training, July, University of Wyoming, Laramie.

———. 1982. "An Intensive Summer Workshop for Foreign Teaching Assistants: A Pilot Project." *TESOL Newsletter* 16(3): 31.

Smith, Rosslyn M., and C. Len Ainsworth. 1987. "It's Working: A Training Program for Foreign Teaching Assistants." In *To Improve the Academy*, edited by Joanne Kurfiss. A joint publication of the Professional and Organizational Development Network in Higher Education and the National Council for Staff, Program, and Organizational Development. Stillwater, Okla.: New Forums Press, Inc.

Smith, Rosslyn M., Patricia Byrd, Janet C. Constantinides, and Ralph Pat Barrett. 1991. "Instructional Development Programs for International TAs: A Systems Analysis Approach." In *To Improve the Academy*, edited by Kenneth J. Zahorski. Professional and Organizational Development Network in Higher Education. Stillwater, Okla.: New Forums Press, Inc.

Smith, Rosslyn, Janet C. Constantinides, and Linda Hudson. 1989. "Orientation: Improving Interaction Between American Students and International Teaching Assistants." Workshop presented at the NAFSA Conference, May, Minneapolis.

Smith, Rosslyn (producer), and Mark Slusher (editor). 1988. *You and the International TA: Paths to Better Understanding*. Videotape. Lubbock, Texas: KTXT-TV, Channel 5 and Washington, D.C.: NAFSA.

Smoch, Richard, and Robert J. Menges. 1985. "Programs for TAs in the Context of Campus Policies and Priorities." In *Strengthening the Teaching Assistant Faculty*, edited by John Andrews. New Directions for Teaching and Learning No. 22. San Francisco: Jossey-Bass.

Soppelsa, Elizabeth. January 1985. "Becoming An Effective Graduate Teaching Assistant in the U.S." *Overseas Counselors' Newsletter.* 28-31.

SPEAK: Speaking Proficiency English Assessment Kit. 1992. Princeton, N.J.: Educational Testing Service.

Stansfield, Charles W., and Rodney J. Ballard. 1984. "Two Instruments for Assessing the Oral English Proficiency of Foreign Teaching Assistants." In *Foreign Teaching Assistants in U.S. Universities*, edited by Kathleen M. Bailey, Frank Pialorsi, and Jean Zukowski-Faust. Washington, D.C.: NAFSA.

Steen, Lynn Arthur, ed. 1987. *Calculus for a New Century: A Pump, Not a Filter.* MAA Notes No. 8. Washington, D.C.: Mathematical Association of America.

Stelzner, Sara Latham. 1987. "Peer Training in a Teaching Improvement Program for TAs." In *Institutional Responsibilities and Responses in the Employment and Education of Teaching Assistants: Readings from a National Conference*, edited by Nancy Van Note Chism and Susan Warner. Columbus: Center for Teaching Excellence, The Ohio State University.

Stenson, Nancy, Bruce Downing, Jan Smith, and Karin Smith. 1991. "Computer-assisted Accent Reduction: Is It Effective?" Paper presented at the TESOL Convention, March, New York.

Stevens, Scott G. 1988. "Improving the International Teaching Assistant Experience: An Evaluative Study of a Training Program." Ph.D. dissertation, University of Delaware.

———. 1989. "A 'Dramatic' Approach to Improving the Intelligibility of ITAs." *English for Specific Purposes* 8: 181-94.

Swales, John, and Patricia L. Rounds. 1985. *College Classroom Discourse.* Ann Arbor: English Language Institute, University of Michigan. Accompanying videotape.

Swanbeck, H. October 26, 1981. "Foreign TAs Experience Communication Gap in Classroom." *Daily Bruin*: 1+.

Tanner, Mark W. 1991a. "Incorporating Research on Question-Asking into ITA Training." In *Preparing the Professoriate of Tomorrow to Teach: Selected Readings in TA Training*, edited by Jody D. Nyquist, Robert D. Abbott, Donald H. Wulff, and Jo Sprague. Dubuque, Iowa: Kendall-Hunt Publishing Company.

————. 1991b. "NNSTA-Student Interaction: An Analysis of TAs' Questions and Students' Responses in a Laboratory Setting." Ph.D. dissertation, University of Pennsylvania.

Taylor, Sally. 1987. "The Student Instructor Program at Brigham Young University." In *Institutional Responsibilities and Responses in the Employment and Education of Teaching Assistants: Readings from a National Conference*, edited by Nancy Van Note Chism and Susan Warner. Columbus: Center for Teaching Excellence, The Ohio State University.

Texas Education Code Section 51.917, amended 1989 by HB638.

Thomas, Clayton F., and Patricia K. Monoson. 1991. "Issues Related to State-mandated English Language Proficiency Requirements." In *Preparing the Professoriate of Tomorrow to Teach: Selected Readings in TA Training*, edited by Jody D. Nyquist, Robert D. Abbott, Donald H. Wulff, and Jo Sprague. Dubuque, Iowa: Kendall-Hunt Publishing Company.

————. 1992. "Factors Which Predict Oral English Language Proficiency Policy Development." Paper presented at the TESOL Convention, March, Vancouver, British Columbia.

Timmerman, M. May 4, 1981. "Foreign Profs' Language Barrier Irritates Students." *Daily Bruin*: np.

Tipton, Sara. June 1990. "ITA Training: How One Trainer Approaches the Challenge." *TESOL Newsletter*.

"Today's Multicultural Reality." 1992. In *International Atlanta 1992*. Atlanta: Atlanta Chamber of Commerce.

Turitz, Nina J. 1984. "A Survey of Training Programs for Foreign Teaching Assistants in American Universities." In *Foreign Teaching Assistants in U.S. Universities*, edited by Kathleen M. Bailey, Frank Pialorsi, and Jean Zukowski-Faust. Washington, D.C.: NAFSA.

Turner, Jean, and Janet Goodwin. 1988. "Placement Testing for International TA Training Programs: Who Needs What?" Paper presented at the Symposium on the Training of International Teaching Assistants, April, University of Pennsylvania, Philadelphia.

Tyler, Andrea, and Catherine Davies. 1990. "Cross-Linguistic Communication Missteps." *Text* 10: 385-411.

Tyler, Andrea E., Ann A. Jeffries, and Catherine E. Davies. 1988. "The Effect of Discourse Devices on Listener Perceptions of Coherence in Non-Native University Teacher's Spoken Discourse." *World Englishes* 7: 101-10.

"UI Senate Discusses Foreign TAs." May 4, 1986. *The Champaign-Urbana News Gazette*: A13.

Veysey, Lawrence R. 1965. *The Emergence of the American University*. Chicago: University of Chicago Press.

vom Saal, Diane R. 1987. "The Undergraduate Experience and International Teaching Assistants." In *Institutional Responsibilities and Responses in the Employment and Education of Teaching Assistants: Readings from a National Conference*, edited by Nancy Van Note Chism and Susan Warner. Columbus: Center for Teaching Excellence, The Ohio State University.

vom Saal, Diane, R.J. Miles, and R.L. McGraw. 1988. "A University-Wide Assessment and Training Program for International Teaching Assistants." *Journal of Agronomic Education* 17(2): 68-72.

Weimer, Maryellen, Marilla D. Svinicki, and Gabriele Bauer. 1989. "Designing Programs to Prepare TAs to Teach." In *Teaching Assistant Training in the 1990s*, edited by Jody D. Nyquist, Robert D. Abbott, and Donald H. Wulff. New Directions for Teaching and Learning No. 39. San Francisco: Jossey- Bass.

Wennerstrom, Ann. 1989a. "ITA Training: Pronunciation on the Job." Demonstration presented at the TESOL Convention, March, San Antonio, Texas.

———. 1989b. *Techniques for Teachers*. A companion workbook to the videotape *Techniques for Teachers: A Guide for Non-Native Speakers of English*. Seattle: University of Washington Extension.

Will, W. Marvin. 1980. "American Politics in Comparative Perspective: Thoughts on Teaching the Course to International Students." *Teaching Political Science* 7(4): 473-80.

Williams, J., Gregory A. Barnes, Alexis G. Finger, and Patrick J. Ruffin. 1987. "Training FTAs: Report of a Needs Analysis." Paper presented at the TESOL Convention, April, Miami. ED 289 436. MF-01; PC-01.

Wolcowitz, J. 1982. "The First Day of Class." In *The Art and Craft of Teaching*, edited by Margaret M. Gullette. Cambridge, Mass.: Harvard-Danforth Center for Teaching and Learning.

Wulff, Donald H., Ann Q. Staton-Spicer, Carla W. Hess, and Jody D. Nyquist. 1985. *The Student Perspective on Evaluating Teaching Effectiveness*. Seattle: Center for Instructional Development and Research, University of Washington.

Young, Richard, ed. 1989. *English for Specific Purposes* 7(1).

———. 1990. "Curriculum Renewal in Training Programs for International Teaching Assistants." *Journal of Intensive English Studies* 4: 59-77. ED 317 067. MF-01; PC-01.

Yule, George. 1991. "Developing Communicative Effectiveness Through the Negotiated Resolution of Referential Conflicts." *Linguistics and Education* 5: 31-45.

Yule, George, and Paul Hoffman. 1990. "Predicting Success for ITAs in a U.S. University." *TESOL Quarterly* 24: 227-43.

INDEX

A

AAUP (American Association of University Professors), 17

Adelman study. See history of undergraduate education.

African American doctoral students. See discrimination against minorities

Assessment of TAs'. See also oral proficiency and screening tests

 end-of-term student instructional ratings, 48-49

 end-of-term evaluations by TA supervisor, 49-50

 external evaluations, 47

 in-class observations, 49

 peer evaluation, 47-48, 50-51

 self-evaluation, 51

 structured self-evaluation, 48

C

Chinese academic culture. See response to questions

 TA classroom behavior, 72

 TA speech patterns cause confusion, 71-72

City College of the City University of New York, 29

Columbia University, 40

Cornell University, 47

CGS (Council of Graduate Schools), 17

concerns of International Teaching Assistants, 78-79

content change to meet non-English background needs, 10-11

courses

 percentage taken by institution type, 8

 percentage taken in certain fields of study, 7

 taken by 20% or more of students, 6

 taken by undergraduates, 5

cultural audit. See systems analysis

Curricular Components, 37-42. See also topics required in training programs

 design questions, 37

 necessary skills, 37-38

D

deficiencies of international teaching assistants (ITA) in

 cross-cultural communication, xvii, 17

 educational background, 22

 pedagogy, 17

 poor English skills, xvii, 15, 22

deficiencies of international teaching assistants (ITA) response to

 institutional. See Institutional ITA assessment

 legislative, 15-16

 national conferences on. See presentations on testing & training

 of public, 15

 student background affects perception, 26-27

testing and training, 17

discrimination against minorities, 12

dissertations on testing and training, 19. See also search strategies

Drexel University, 42, 58

E

Emory University, 56, 57

environmental scan. See systems analysis

evaluation of training programs, 62-66

    comparison of evaluation items, 65-66

    end-of-term student instructional rating survey, 63-64

    evaluation of level of attainment, 65

    survey of TA/ITA participants and program staff, 64

    survey of the TAs' departments, 65

F

faculty development, 21

Foreign Teaching Assistants in American Universities, 19

G

Georgia State University, 57

I

international faculty in U.S., 9

Institute on Foreign TA Training. See Wyoming/NAPSA Institute

Institutional ITA assessment. See also training programs

    criticism of policy, 20

    faculty objections, 20

    ignoring the issue, 19

    legislative mandates, 20

international student body

    growth after World War II, 1

    problems of definition, 4

    small percentage of total student body, 3

Iowa State University, 57

K

Korean TA speech patterns cause confusion, 71-72

M

Michigan State University, 37, 47, 58

Mississippi State University, 28, 57

N

NAFSA (Association of International Educators), 17

national conference on teaching assistants, 18

non-European U.S. immigrant population increase, 9

O

Ohio State University, 18, 57
oral proficiency tests
    communicative performance, 57-58
    interview, 55-56
    SPEAK, 53-55
    teaching simulation, 56-57
    telephone interview, 53
    test of English as a foreign language (TOEFL), 52, 74
    test of Spoken English (TSE), 52-53

P

Pennsylvania State University, 34, 37, 54-55
performance studies, 77-78
"policy papers," 20
presentations on testing and training, 17-19
program designs, 27-37
    concurrent, 30
    orientation, 28
    pre-term orientation, 28-29
    pre-term orientation with follow-up, 29-30
    pre-term/pre-teach, 30-33
    pre-term/pre-teach with follow-up, 33-34
    term-long concurrent, 34
    term-long concurrent pre-teach, 35
    term-long concurrent while teaching, 35-36
pronunciation
    computer assisted instruction, 39
    studies of, 68-70
    teaching, 39

R

research categories, 68-79
research needs, 82
    assessment and training for international faculty, 84-85
    characteristics of the undergraduate classroom, 82-83
    effectiveness of ITA training and assessment, 83
    institutional policy development regarding ITA training, 85
    intercultural orientation of U.S. undergraduate, 84
    possible conflicts caused for the ITA by training, 83-84
research universities
    structural contradictions, 1
    merits of research versus teaching, 11
    discord over demands for change, 12
    struggle between faculty and administration, 12-13
response to questions, 22

S

science, technology and business administration U.S. student decrease, 2

screening tests, 58-62
      pre-training, pre-teaching, 58-60
      post-training, 60
      concurrent-with-training, 61

search strategies for research related to ITA training
      examination of appropriate databases, 67-68
      check for doctoral dissertations, 68
      consult published collections of papers, 68
      manual search of national publications, 68

Seattle conference on teaching assistants, 18

SIETAR (Society for Intercultural Education, Training, and Research), 17

Southern Illinois University, 56

systems analysis, 23

T

Taiwanese TA classroom behavior. See Chinese TA classroom behavior

teacher effectiveness measurement, 70-74

teaching assistants
      classroom instruction, 21
      increase in numbers from non-Western traditions, 2
      need, xvii
      practice common to hire new international students as, 7
      selection criteria, 11
      value, xvii

teaching effectiveness studies, 70-74

teaching staff mandatory testing, 15-16, 84
      discriminatory implications, 16
      in Florida, 16
      in Ohio, 16
      in Oklahoma, 15-16
      States with laws on in 1992, 16

tests.
      see oral proficiency tests
      see screening tests
      see teaching staff mandatory testing

TESOL (Teachers of English to Speakers of Other Languages), 17, 19

Texas international staff training costs, 26

Texas Tech University, 26, 32-33, 41-43, 57

The International Teaching Assistant, 18

topics required in training programs, 38-42
      culture, 40-41
      curriculum. See also curricular components

diversity in the classroom, 42
laboratory safety, 42
language, 38-40
micro-teaching practice, 41-42
pedagogy, 40
sexual harassment, 42
training costs. See training programs-funding
training programs, 19-20.
administration, 24-25
administrative support required, 85-86
assessment. See evaluation of training programs.
availability, 25-26
background, xvii, 21-22
curriculum. See curricular components
designing an appropriate program, 23
designs. See program designs
evaluation research, 75-77
facilities, 26
faculty and staff, 26
funding, 25-26
future prospects, 86-87
implementation (enforcement, notification, materials),
    42-44
international faculty for, 44-45
rationale, 23-24
research related to. See search strategies for
topics. See topics required in training programs

U
undergraduates
courses taken by, 5
history of education of, 5-10
teaching assistants influence on, 4
University of
California at Berkeley, 47
California at Los Angeles, 58
Delaware pre-term/pre-teach program, 30-31
Illinois at Urbana-Champaign, 28
Iowa, 57
Kentucky, 57
Maryland, 57
Michigan, 37, 44, 57, 58
Minnesota, 57
Missouri-Columbia pre-term/pre-teach program, 31
Nebraska-Lincoln, 33
Nevada orientation with follow-up, 30
Nevada-Reno, 56, 57
Oklahoma, 57

Pennsylvania, 18, 42, 58.
Pittsburgh, 56, 58
South Dakota, 56
Texas-Austin, 58
Toledo, 57
Washington, 37, 44
Wyoming, 24, 32-33, 37, 43, 56, 57

V
Vanderbilt University, 57

W
Wayne State University, 57
women and minorities—adverse influence of teaching assistants
  on, 12
Wyoming/NAPSA Institute, 18-19

ASHE-ERIC HIGHER EDUCATION REPORTS

Since 1983, the Association for the Study of Higher Education (ASHE) and the Educational Resources Information Center (ERIC) Clearinghouse on Higher Education, a sponsored project of the School of Education and Human Development at The George Washington University, have cosponsored the *ASHE-ERIC Higher Education Report* series. The 1992 series is the twenty-first overall and the fourth to be published by the School of Education and Human Development at the George Washington University.

Each monograph is the definitive analysis of a tough higher education problem, based on thorough research of pertinent literature and institutional experiences. Topics are identified by a national survey. Noted practitioners and scholars are then commissioned to write the reports, with experts providing critical reviews of each manuscript before publication.

Eight monographs (10 before 1985) in the ASHE-ERIC Higher Education Report series are published each year and are available on individual and subscription bases. Subscription to eight issues is $90.00 annually; $70 to members of AAHE, AIR, or AERA; and $60 to ASHE members. All foreign subscribers must include an additional $10 per series year for postage.

To order, use the order form on the last page of this book. Regular prices, and special rates available to members of AAHE, AIR, AERA and ASHE, are as follows:

Series	Regular	Members
1990 to 92	$17.00	$12.75
1988 and 89	15.00	11.25
1985 to 87	10.00	7.50
1983 and 84	7.50	6.00
before 1983	6.50	5.00

Shipping costs are as follows:
- U.S. address: 5% of invoice subtotal for orders over $50.00; $2.50 for each order with an invoice subtotal of $50.00 or less.
- Foreign: $2.50 per book.

All orders under $45.00 must be prepaid. Make check payable to ASHE-ERIC. For Visa or MasterCard, include card number, expiration date and signature. A bulk discount of 10% is available on orders of 10 or more books, and 20% on orders of 25 or more books (not applicable on subscriptions).

Address order to
ASHE-ERIC Higher Education Reports
The George Washington University
1 Dupont Circle, Suite 630
Washington, DC 20036
Or phone (202) 296-2597
Write or call for a complete catalog.

1992 ASHE-ERIC Higher Education Reports

1. The Leadership Compass: Values and Ethics in Higher Education
   John R. Wilcox and Susan L. Ebbs

2. Preparing for a Global Community: Achieving an International Perspective in Higher Education
   Sarah M. Pickert

3. Quality: Transforming Postsecondary Education
   Ellen Earle Chaffee and Lawrence A. Sherr

4. Faculty Job Satisfaction: Women and Minorities in Peril
   Martha Wingard Tack and Carol Logan Patitu

5. Reconciling Rights and Responsibilities of Colleges and Students: Offensive Speech, Assembly, Drug Testing, and Safety
   Annette Gibbs

6. Creating Distinctiveness: Lessons from Uncommon Colleges and Universities
   Barbara K. Townsend, L. Jackson Newell, and Michael D. Wiese

7. Instituting Enduring Innovations: Achieving Continuity of Change in Higher Education
   Barbara K. Curry

1991 ASHE-ERIC Higher Education Reports

1. Active Learning: Creating Excitement in the Classroom
   Charles C. Bonwell and James A. Eison

2. Realizing Gender Equality in Higher Education: The Need to Integrate Work/Family Issues
   Nancy Hensel

3. Academic Advising for Student Success: A System of Shared Responsibility
   Susan H. Frost

4. Cooperative Learning: Increasing College Faculty Instructional Productivity
   David W. Johnson, Roger T. Johnson, and Karl A. Smith

5. High School–College Partnerships: Conceptual Models, Programs, and Issues
   Arthur Richard Greenberg

6. Meeting the Mandate: Renewing the College and Departmental Curriculum
   William Toombs and William Tierney

7. Faculty Collaboration: Enhancing the Quality of Scholarship and Teaching
   Ann E. Austin and Roger G. Baldwin

8. Strategies and Consequences: Managing the Costs in Higher Education
   John S. Waggaman

1990 ASHE-ERIC Higher Education Reports

1. The Campus Green: Fund Raising in Higher Education
   Barbara E. Brittingham and Thomas R. Pezzullo

2. The Emeritus Professor: Old Rank - New Meaning
   James E. Mauch, Jack W. Birch, and Jack Matthews

3. "High Risk" Students in Higher Education: Future Trends
   Dionne J. Jones and Betty Collier Watson

4. Budgeting for Higher Education at the State Level: Enigma, Paradox, and Ritual
   Daniel T. Layzell and Jan W. Lyddon

5. Proprietary Schools: Programs, Policies, and Prospects
   John B. Lee and Jamie P. Merisotis

6. College Choice: Understanding Student Enrollment Behavior
   Michael B. Paulsen

7. Pursuing Diversity: Recruiting College Minority Students
   Barbara Astone and Elsa Nuñez-Wormack

8. Social Consciousness and Career Awareness: Emerging Link in Higher Education
   John S. Swift, Jr.

1989 ASHE-ERIC Higher Education Reports

1. Making Sense of Administrative Leadership: The 'L' Word in Higher Education
   Estela M. Bensimon, Anna Neumann, and Robert Birnbaum

2. Affirmative Rhetoric, Negative Action: African-American and Hispanic Faculty at Predominantly White Universities
   Valora Washington and William Harvey

3. Postsecondary Developmental Programs: A Traditional Agenda with New Imperatives
   Louise M. Tomlinson

4. The Old College Try: Balancing Athletics and Academics in Higher Education
   John R. Thelin and Lawrence L. Wiseman

5. The Challenge of Diversity: Involvement or Alienation in the Academy?
   Daryl G. Smith

6. Student Goals for College and Courses: A Missing Link in Assessing and Improving Academic Achievement
   Joan S. Stark, Kathleen M. Shaw, and Malcolm A. Lowther

7. The Student as Commuter: Developing a Comprehensive Institutional Response
   Barbara Jacoby

8. Renewing Civic Capacity: Preparing College Students for Service and Citizenship
   Suzanne W. Morse

1988 ASHE-ERIC Higher Education Reports

1. The Invisible Tapestry: Culture in American Colleges and Universities
   George D. Kuh and Elizabeth J. Whitt

2. Critical Thinking: Theory, Research, Practice, and Possibilities
   Joanne Gainen Kurfiss

3. Developing Academic Programs: The Climate for Innovation
   Daniel T. Seymour

4. Peer Teaching: To Teach is To Learn Twice
   Neal A. Whitman

5. Higher Education and State Governments: Renewed Partnership, Cooperation, or Competition?
   Edward R. Hines

6. Entrepreneurship and Higher Education: Lessons for Colleges, Universities, and Industry
   James S. Fairweather

7. Planning for Microcomputers in Higher Education: Strategies for the Next Generation
   Reynolds Ferrante, John Hayman, Mary Susan Carlson, and Harry Phillips

8. The Challenge for Research in Higher Education: Harmonizing Excellence and Utility
   Alan W. Lindsay and Ruth T. Neumann

1987 ASHE-ERIC Higher Education Reports

1. Incentive Early Retirement Programs for Faculty: Innovative Responses to a Changing Environment
   Jay L. Chronister and Thomas R. Kepple, Jr.

2. Working Effectively with Trustees: Building Cooperative Campus Leadership
   Barbara E. Taylor

3. Formal Recognition of Employer-Sponsored Instruction: Conflict and Collegiality in Postsecondary Education
   Nancy S. Nash and Elizabeth M. Hawthorne

4. Learning Styles: Implications for Improving Educational Practices
   Charles S. Claxton and Patricia H. Murrell

5. Higher Education Leadership: Enhancing Skills through Professional Development Programs
   Sharon A. McDade

6. Higher Education and the Public Trust: Improving Stature in Colleges and Universities
   Richard L. Alfred and Julie Weissman

7. College Student Outcomes Assessment: A Talent Development Perspective
   Maryann Jacobi, Alexander Astin, and Frank Ayala, Jr.

8. Opportunity from Strength: Strategic Planning Clarified with Case Examples
   Robert G. Cope

1986 ASHE-ERIC Higher Education Reports

1. Post-tenure Faculty Evaluation: Threat or Opportunity?
   Christine M. Licata

2. Blue Ribbon Commissions and Higher Education: Changing Academe from the Outside
   Janet R. Johnson and Laurence R. Marcus

3. Responsive Professional Education: Balancing Outcomes and Opportunities
   Joan S. Stark, Malcolm A. Lowther, and Bonnie M.K. Hagerty

4. Increasing Students' Learning: A Faculty Guide to Reducing Stress among Students
   Neal A. Whitman, David C. Spendlove, and Claire H. Clark

5. Student Financial Aid and Women: Equity Dilemma?
   Mary Moran

6. The Master's Degree: Tradition, Diversity, Innovation
   Judith S. Glazer

7. The College, the Constitution, and the Consumer Student: Implications for Policy and Practice
   Robert M. Hendrickson and Annette Gibbs

8. Selecting College and University Personnel: The Quest and the Question
   Richard A. Kaplowitz

1985 ASHE-ERIC Higher Education Reports

1. Flexibility in Academic Staffing: Effective Policies and Practices
   Kenneth P. Mortimer, Marque Bagshaw, and Andrew T. Masland

2. Associations in Action: The Washington, D.C. Higher Education
   Community
   Harland G. Bloland

3. And on the Seventh Day: Faculty Consulting and Supplemental
   Income
   Carol M. Boyer and Darrell R. Lewis

4. Faculty Research Performance: Lessons from the Sciences and
   Social Sciences
   John W. Creswell

5. Academic Program Review: Institutional Approaches, Expectations, and Controversies
   Clifton F. Conrad and Richard F. Wilson

6. Students in Urban Settings: Achieving the Baccalaureate Degree
   Richard C. Richardson, Jr. and Louis W. Bender

7. Serving More Than Students: A Critical Need for College Student
   Personnel Services
   Peter H. Garland

8. Faculty Participation in Decision Making: Necessity or Luxury?
   Carol E. Floyd

*Out-of-print. Available through EDRS. Call 1-800-443-ERIC.

ORDER FORM 92-8

Quantity **Amount**

_____ Please begin my subscription to the 1992 *ASHE-ERIC Higher Education Reports* at $90.00, 33% off the cover price, starting with Report 1, 1992.   _____

_____ Please send a complete set of the 1991 *ASHE-ERIC Higher Education Reports* at $80.00, 41% off the cover price.   _____

_____ Outside the U.S., add $10.00 per series for postage.   _____

Individual reports are avilable at the following prices:

1990 to 1992, $17.00	1983 and 1984, $7.50
1988 and 1989, $15.00	1982 and back, $6.50
1985 to 1987, $10.00	

SHIPPING: **U.S. Orders:** *For subtotal (before discount) of $50.00 or less, add $2.50. For subtotal over $50.00, add 5% of subtotal. Call for rush service options.* **Foreign Orders:** *$2.50 per book.* **U.S. Subscriptions:** *Included in price.* **Foreign Subscriptions:** *Add $10.00*

PLEASE SEND ME THE FOLLOWING REPORTS:

Quantity	Report No.	Year	Title	Amount

Subtotal:	
Shipping:	
Total Due:	

Please check one of the following:
☐ Check enclosed, payable to GWU–ERIC.
☐ Purchase order attached ($45.00 minimum).
☐ Charge my credit card indicated below:
    ☐ Visa   ☐ MasterCard

Expiration Date _____

Name _____

Title _____

Institution _____

Address _____

City _____ State _____ Zip _____

Phone _____ Fax _____ Telex _____

Signature _____ Date _____

SEND ALL ORDERS TO:
ASHE-ERIC Higher Education Reports
The George Washington University
One Dupont Circle, Suite 630
Washington, DC 20036-1183
Phone: (202) 296-2597